2022

QUANTUM HUMAN DESIGN EVOLUTION GUIDE

Using Solar Transits To Design Your Year

KAREN CURRY PARKER

An Imprint for GracePoint Publishing (www.GracePointPublishing.com)

GracePoint Matrix, LLC
624 S. Cascade Ave
Suite 201
Colorado Springs, CO 80903
www.GracePointMatrix.com
Email: Admin@GracePointMatrix.com
SAN # 991-6032

A Library of Congress Control Number has been requested and is pending.

ISBN: (Paperback) 978-1-955272-07-0
eISBN: 978-1-955272-08-7

Books may be purchased for educational, business, or sales promotional use.
For bulk order requests and price schedule contact:
Orders@GracePointPublishing.com

2022

QUANTUM HUMAN DESIGN
EVOLUTION GUIDE
Using Solar Transits to Design Your Year
KAREN CURRY PARKER

Please visit QuantumAlignmentSystem.com for more information about Quantum Human Design, to see a list of our Certified Specialists, and for additional valuable resources.

Follow Karen and Quantum Human Design across social media platforms:
@KarenCurryParker

To all my students, Quantum Human Design Specialists, and Quantum Alignment Practitioners: Thank you for trusting me to be your teacher. Thank you for sharing the gift of Who You Truly Are with the world. I am because you are. I love you!

CONTENTS

INTRODUCTION

This book is a weekly guide designed to give you a deliberate way to harness the energy of the Sun and the Moon to support you in creating what you want in your life.

Quantum Human Design is a collection of cross-cultural, ancient and modern archetypes. An archetype is a pattern of thought or symbolic image that is derived from the past collective experience of humanity.

We experience all of the archetypes in the Human Design charts, either from our own unique charts, our relationships, or through the planetary transits. In other words, we all have all of the chart. We just experience the archetypes of the chart differently depending on the unique configuration of our individual charts.

The colored in or "defined" elements in your Human Design chart tell you which archetypes you carry in your own chart. The "defined" elements in your chart are part of what you must conquer to bring your gifts into the world. These energies represent your soul curriculum, what you're here to learn over the course of your life.

The white or "undefined" elements in your Human Design chart tell you a lot about what you are here to learn from others and from the world. You will experience these archetypes in a variety of different ways depending on who you are with and what energies are transiting in the celestial weather. The undefined elements of your chart represent the themes you are designed to explore through your relationships with others and your interactions with the world.

Over the course of a calendar year, the Sun moves through all 64 of the Human Design Gates. The Human Design Gates contain the energy code for 64 core human archetypes. As the sun moves through an archetype, it "lights up" that theme for everyone on the planet, creating a theme for the week.

We all deal with the weekly themes. Even if the theme doesn't impact your chart deeply, it will impact the charts of the people around you. The gift of the solar transits is that it gives you an opportunity to work deliberately with all 64 of these core human archetypes and to consciously focus on living the highest expression of these energies in your daily life. The solar transits also bring you creative energies that help you meet the goals you set for yourself each year.

The moon in Human Design represents the energy of what drives us. In traditional astrology, the new moon phase and the full moon phase represent bookend energies that mark the beginning and the end of a monthly creative cycle.

The new moon helps us set the intention for our goals for the month. The full moon supports us in releasing any energies, beliefs, or blocks that are hindering the completion of our goals.

Lunar and solar eclipses are bookends that mark beginnings and endings. The work we do in between can be powerful, and both internal, as well as external. Eclipse energy represents cycles that support you in aligning more deeply with your bigger goals in life, and support you in breaking free from habits and patterns that keep you from growing and expanding.

To learn more about the transits and how they affect your personal Human Design chart and your energy click here:

http://www.freehumandesignchart.com

HOW TO USE THIS BOOK

The 2022 Quantum Human Design Evolution Guide is a workbook with journal questions, affirmations, and Emotional Freedom Techniques (EFT) setup phrases for every gate as the sun moves through them. If you are not a fan of journaling, feel free to contemplate the prompts in whatever way works for you. You may walk with them, meditate on them, or even discuss them with your friends.

I am excited to share with you updated Quantum Human Design™ language. Over the years it has become obvious to me the vocabulary in Human Design is in need of an upgrade in response to evolutionary shifts and with respect to new research that shows how the language we use is so powerful, it can even change your DNA. I hope you enjoy the new language!

Each of the Human Design Gates has a "challenge" associated with it. This is what you must conquer to get the most out of the movement of the Sun which occurs approximately every six days. Before you complete the writing assignment, read the "challenge" for each Gate and contemplate what you need to do to get the most out of each of the weekly archetypes.

The Emotional Freedom Techniques is a powerful energy psychology tool that has been scientifically proven to change your emotional, mental, and genetic programming to help you express your highest potential. Each week you may work with a specific EFT setup phrase to help you clear any old energies you may be carrying related to the archetype of the week. (Learn more about how to use EFT here: www.quantumalignmentsystem.com/solar-transit-calendar)

You will also find exercises for each new moon, full moon, solar eclipse, and lunar eclipse complete with a writing/contemplation assignment and affirmation. You will be guided in working with the theme of the lunar cycles and eclipses so that you can make the most of these powerful energy cycles.

Every Human Design year gives us a 365-day creative cycle that supports us in releasing what no longer serves us, allows us to consciously increase our creative energy, grow, and evolve with the support of the stars.

May you have a prosperous and joyful 2022!

THE THEME OF THE YEAR

2022: The Year of Healing the Karma of Power, Personal Conviction, and the Responsibility of the Individual to the Whole

I don't like starting my summary of the year ahead with a cautionary note, especially the same cautionary note that I started with last year, but I think it is vital we enter the new year with the awareness that we are in the beginning of a revolution that started in late 2019 and promises to continue until 2024. Patience and the ability to sustain and endure are essential.

I want to gently remind you that the celestial weather and cycles of the next few years are bringing us essential energy to help us build an equitable, sustainable, and peaceful world. We cannot just imagine and wish for a better world. We must do the inner and outer work of dismantling old structures, destroying outdated beliefs, and demolishing the institutions and systems that no longer reflect our evolved understanding of the inherent value and beauty of all life on the planet.

I want to start this year's Evolution Guide with a quick overview of the Nodes and the themes they are setting us up for this year. The Nodes set the theme or the "plot outline" for our personal and collective narrative. The South Node represents what we need to understand and learn from in order to move into the theme of the North Node.

In September of 2021, the Nodes began a long journey highlighting Gates in the Individual Circuitry (Transformational Circuitry in Quantum Human Design™). The Nodes continue to highlight Gates in the Individual Circuit until 2024.

What does that mean?

This means that the themes of the Individual Circuit will be highlighted for all of us for the next three years.

There are three kinds of circuits in Human Design: Individual (Transformation in Quantum Human Design), Tribal (Sustainability in Quantum Human Design), and Collective (Synergy in Quantum Human Design. Each Circuit plays an essential role in the evolution of humanity.

Individual Circuitry brings mutation and change. Tribal Circuity explores and implements the ideas brought in by the Individual Circuit and, once the change has demonstrated that it is functional and adaptable, it is integrated into the Collective.

Think of it like this. Imagine that there are two caveman brothers, Bob and Tom. Bob is a little weird and strange. He tries his whole life to fit in, but no one really "gets" him. Bob moves out of his family group and makes a home on his own by the edge of fruitful river a mile or so away from his family where he is very happy to be free to do his own thing.

Tom is very different from his brother, Bob. Tom has a deep sense of being rooted in his family group and works tirelessly to make sure that his family has everything they need to be healthy and abundant. This includes his brother, Bob. Once a week, Tom travels to visit Bob at his home by the river to make sure Bob is okay and thriving. Both brothers enjoy their weekly meeting because, even though they are very different, they deeply love each other.

One week Tom notices that Bob is using a cool tool that he invented that makes construction and work much easier. Tom studies the tool and decides to make his own when he gets home to his family group.

The tool is so popular and makes work so much easier that soon all of his family group have made their own and are using the tool to make building shelters and gathering fruit easier.

In the fall, Tom travels with extra food and supplies over the hill to a gathering place with other leaders from different family groups. He brings his new tool with him. Other leaders from the different family groups see Tom using his new tool and make their own, bringing this new invention to their own family groups.

Soon, the leaders of the different family groups gather and decide that this tool is incredibly valuable and that all known family groups far and wide should have access to this powerful tool because it saves so much time, energy, and effort. They create a committee to make the tools and to travel around the area delivering the tools to different family groups and increasing the quality of life everywhere they travel.

Bob represents the core theme of the Individual Circuit. He doesn't quite fit in. He has his own ideas. He stays true to those ideas and travels on his own on a journey of self-exploration and self-expression.

Bob's new ideas and insights profoundly influence Tom, who represents Tribal Circuitry. Tom is deeply occupied with exploring what would make the people he loves happy and safe. He takes great joy in nurturing others and his contribution makes everyone around him feel loved and safe.

The leaders from the other family groups who enable new legislation for the "tool" represent Collective Circuitry. Their joint actions create initiatives that not only make their own family groups safer and more sustainable, but they also work to ensure that others have the same opportunities for growth and access to resources.

This is an idealized version of how all the circuits work together. Let me remind us all that we all have all of the Gates and Circuits, just some of them are defined (colored in) and some are open (white). We all have Gates from all of the Circuits defined in our charts.

Some of us are more profoundly influenced by the themes of the different Circuits. If you have Channels in a particular Circuit defined in your chart, it will most likely give you the theme of that particular circuit in your life story.

Traditional Human Design teaches that Individual Circuitry does not "care." I think this teaching gets wildly misinterpreted and to really understand the evolutionary tasks at hand, we must be extraordinarily clear about the meaning of the verb, *to care*.

Essential definition of the verb *to care*:

> 1: effort made to do something correctly, safely, or without causing damage
> She used care in selecting a doctor for her son.
> a box marked Handle With Care [=handle carefully]
>
> 2: things that are done to keep someone healthy, safe, etc.
> The children have inadequate medical care and little formal education.
> We need to provide people experiencing economic hardship with better dental care.
>
> 3: things that are done to keep something in good condition
> She wrote a book about car care.
> With proper care, the machine should last a decade or more.

Somehow in the interpretation of the phrase, "Individuality doesn't care," we concluded that people with a lot of Individual Circuitry don't have empathy or feelings for other people, have little regard for what others think or experience, and basically can wonder the earth oblivious to the impact of their choices on others.

To be clear, this kind of "not caring" is the shadow expression of the Will Center (Ego), NOT individuality. The Will Center, by the way, is almost exclusively a Tribal Center, all of the Channels connected to the Will Center with the exception of the Channel 25/51, the Channel of Initiation in Quantum Human Design, are Tribal and all about caring. The Channel of Initiation is the Channel that bridges our personal identity (Ego) to the Higher Self.

The "not caring" of the Individual is not about "not caring" about others, it is about not caring about what other people think of your unique way of expressing yourself, your innovative ideas, and your exquisite alignment with your Authentic Self. The ability of the Individual to stay true to their unique, vital, and irreplaceable role in the Cosmic Plan allows the Individual to serve their essential role of bringing change and consequent evolution to the world.

When we live in alignment with our Authentic Self and we claim our personal place in the Cosmic Plan, we live from a place of understanding our value. That recognition of our own personal value enables us to not only claim our own value, but to see the value of others.

It takes tremendous courage and self-worth to fulfill the destiny of Individual Circuitry as well as follow the conviction of your Heart. Cultivating THAT is the challenge facing us over the next few years.

This year tasks us with learning to trust in the timing of the universe. We are conquering waiting patiently and preparing to take action when the timing is right, and keeping our energy occupied while we wait. We are activating our personal empowerment and letting go of playing small, stepping into the unapologetic expression of who we are, and claiming and defending our unique role in the world.

Remember, the role of the Individual is to be themselves because it is from that place of alignment with the Authentic Self, that they show others how to be true to who they are. I agree with this.

Alignment with the Authentic Self creates a high frequency of energy and a state of physiological Heart coherence, which in turn influences your electro-magnetic resonance. All of these states are contagious. When you live true to yourself, you create a wave of energy that lifts others up and encourages them to be in the same energy field of pure self-expression.

Your alignment creates a resonance field that entrains others to be in alignment too, which then spreads to other people and to more people and to other people and so on and so on.

THIS is the power of individuality.

Not only that, fully expressing your Authentic Self and the initiatives that are yours to fulfill, creates phenomenal change and transformation.

Think about Bob.

What would have happened if Bob had denied his own alignment with his Authentic Individual Self. What if he had sucked it up, settled down, and forced himself to fit inside the Tribal box he was born into? What might never have been born into existence if he had failed to follow his true path?

What might never be born into existence if you fail to follow your own true path? That is the question for us to explore and contemplate over the course of 2022.

May this be the year you discover your true power, your vital and irreplaceable role in the Cosmic Plan, and may you boldly proclaim your Right Place in the world!

Have a great year!

From my Heart to Yours,
Karen

ECLIPSE SEASON

The year 2022 features a series of eclipses upon the Taurus-Scorpio axis, a cycle which started in 2021. This eclipse cycle which will last for nearly two years started with a partial lunar eclipse on **Friday, November 19, 2021**, in 27 degrees Taurus and will end on **Saturday, October 28, 2023**.

Taurus is a reliable earth sign, and Scorpio is an emotional water sign. These eclipses upon this axis will push us to put in the work to make our dreams come true and understand which relationships are worthy of our devotion and which ones we should let go of (remember, if we will not end an unhealthy relationship, eclipses tend to do it for us).

This eclipse axis is also giving us an invitation to deepen our faith. Taurus rules nature and all things natural. Scorpio is more about the supernatural realm and invokes the depths of faith and the unseen as part of how it moves through the world. Taurus informs us of a crisis in natural resources and nature crying out for a change. Scorpio comes along and promises us a solution to this crisis if we cultivate the faith that we can and will create an elegant solution.

This continues to work with the energy of Uranus in Taurus, inviting us to disassemble infrastructures that no long support the idea that all life is precious and inherently valuable. Continue to expect this eclipse cycle to keep highlighting what needs to come apart before we can begin the process of restructuring.

Eclipses serve as celestial checkpoints. An eclipse is a high-octane celestial event that helps illuminate our karmic path, but just as these cosmic events can be visually striking, eclipses can also be *a bit* dramatic. Astrologically speaking, they speed up time: They open new doors by slamming others shut, so we often find abrupt and sudden shifts occurring during eclipses.

Though the shifts can be jarring, they can help us by speeding up the inevitable.

If you've been dragging your feet, an eclipse will be sure to give you that extra push (or shove) needed to take action. While the results can be shocking, remember that these celestial events simply expedite the inevitable—these events were going to happen eventually.

Understanding the transits helps you consciously harness the power of the transit and use it to your advantage. This will not necessarily help you avoid the intensity of these catalytic celestial events, but it will help you influence the outcome and better regulate your response to these events. Remember, you cannot always control what happens in your life, but you always have control over what you do with these events.

During Solar Eclipses the Moon is directly between the Earth and Sun, where the Sun and the Moon are said to be in conjunction. For some time, the tiny Moon has the capability to block out the giant Sun by turning off the lights on the earth. This might take away our perspectives in life. Solar eclipses are said to take away fixed patterns and push us into unknown realms. Though this might cause upheavals in our life, they are excellent growth promoters and powerful catalysts.

Below is a list of all the Eclipse dates in this Eclipse cycle, including the Human Design Gates highlighted with each Eclipse:

April 30, 2022 – New Moon and Partial Solar Eclipse

Taurus 10 degrees, 35 minutes – New Moon

Taurus 10 degrees, 27 minutes – Eclipse

Gate 24 – The Gate of Blessings

May 16, 2022 – Full Moon and Lunar Eclipse

Scorpio 25 degrees, 16 minutes – New Moon

Scorpio 25 degrees, 17 minutes – Eclipse

Gate 14 – The Gate of Creation

October 25, 2022 – New Moon and Partial Solar Eclipse

Scorpio 2 degrees, 7 minutes – New Moon

Scorpio 1 degree, 59 minutes – Eclipse

New Moon in Gate 50 – The Gate of Nurturing

Solar Eclipse in Gate 28 – The Gate of Challenge

November 8, 2022 – Full Moon and Lunar Eclipse

Taurus 15 degrees, 59 minutes – Full Moon

Taurus 16 degrees, 00 minutes – Eclipse

Gate 2 – The Gate of Allowing

You will find special Eclipse contemplations in this guide inserted on the dates of the 2022 Eclipse events.

JANUARY 22, 2022

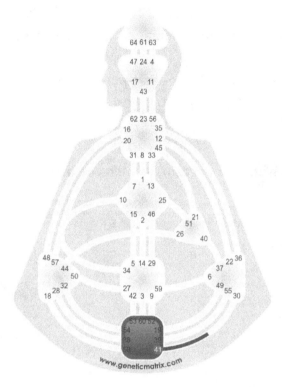

www.geneticmatrix.com

GATE 41: IMAGINATION

CHALLENGE:

To learn to use your imagination as a source of creative inspiration and manifestation. To experience the world and imagine more abundant possibilities. To stay connected to your creative fire.

JOURNAL QUESTIONS:

How do I own my creative power?

How can I deepen my self-honoring of my creative power?

How do I express my creative power?

What do I do to hold to my dreams and visions?

Do I allow myself to dream of good things? Do I believe in miracles?

How can I deepen my faith in the goodness of the world?

AFFIRMATION:

I am a creative nexus of inspiration for the world. My ideas and imaginings inspire people to think beyond their limitations. My ideas stimulate new possibilities in the world. I am a powerful creator; my creative thoughts, ideas, and inspirations set the stage for miracles and possibilities that will change the story of humanity.

EFT SETUP:

Even though I am afraid my dreams won't come true, I deeply and completely love and accept myself.

JANUARY 28, 2022

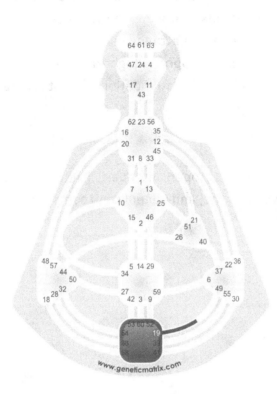

GATE 19: ATTUNEMENT

CHALLENGE:

To learn how to manage being a highly sensitive person and not let your sensitivity cause you to compromise what you want and who you are. To learn to keep your own resources in a sustainable state in order so that you have more to give. To not martyr yourself to the needs of others. To learn how to become emotionally intimate without being shut down or co-dependent.

JOURNAL QUESTIONS:

How do I show up emotionally in my relationships?

Am I emotionally present in my relationships?

How attuned am I to my own emotional needs?

Do I need to ask for more of what I want and need?

AFFIRMATION:

I am deeply aware of the emotional needs and energy of others. My sensitivity and awareness give me insights that allow me to create intimacy and vulnerability in my relationships. I am aware and attuned to the emotional frequency around me and I make adjustments to help support a high frequency of emotional alignment. I honor my own emotional needs as the foundation of what I share with others.

EFT SETUP:

Even though it is scary to open my heart, I now choose to create space for deep intimacy and love in my life, and I deeply and completely love and accept myself.

FEBRUARY 1, 2022 – NEW MOON

 Aquarius 12 degrees, 19 minutes
Gate 19 – The Gate of Attunement

New Moon energy invites us to explore how we can deepen our alignment with our intentions and asks us to focus on what we want to grow and expand on in our lives.

This New Moon is a gentle invitation to explore what stories and narratives you are holding on to that might be blocking you from creating true intimacy in all of your relationships. The story you tell about yourself, your "love-worthiness," and your ability to be supported in a deeply connected way in your partnerships is influencing your experience of partnership and collaboration.

This New Moon encourages you to start telling a better story about what you deserve and value in your relationships. This is a vital time to explore the agreements you are upholding in your relationships, and if these agreements are not aligned with your self-love or self-worth, it is time to write a new set of agreements.

What old stories about being loved and supported do you need to heal, release, or align?

 CHALLENGE:

To learn how to manage being a highly sensitive person and not let your sensitivity cause you to compromise what you want and who you are. To learn to keep your own resources in a sustainable state in order so that you have more to give. To not martyr yourself to the needs of others. To learn how to become emotionally intimate without being shut down or co-dependent.

OPTIMAL EXPRESSION:

The ability to sense the emotional needs of others and your community and know how to bring the emotional energy back into alignment with sufficiency and sustainability. The ability to be emotionally vulnerable and present to increase Heart to Heart connections.

UNBALANCED EXPRESSION:

Being overly sensitive and shutting down or compromising your own needs and wants. Feeling disconnected from others as a way of coping with being overly sensitive. Being emotionally clingy or needy as a way of forcing your natural desire for intimacy.

CONTEMPLATIONS:

How do you manage your sensitivity? What coping mechanisms do you have to keep you emotionally connected in a healthy way?

Are you emotionally present in your relationships? Do you need to become more attuned to your own emotional needs and ask for more of what you want and need?

What emotional patterns do you have that may be causing you to give up what you need and want to fulfill other people's emotional needs?

Are you able to be present to the emotional energy around you to help calibrate in a creative, intimate, and sustainable way?

AFFIRMATION:

I am deeply aware of the emotional needs and energy of others. My sensitivity and awareness give me insights that allow me to create intimacy and vulnerability in my relationships. I am aware and attuned to the emotional frequency around me and I make adjustments to help support a high frequency of emotional alignment. I honor my own emotional needs as the foundation of what I share with others.

FEBRUARY 2, 2022

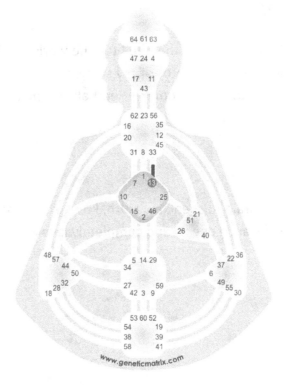

www.geneticmatrix.com

GATE 13: NARRATIVE

CHALLENGE:

To forgive the past and redefine who you are each and every day. To tell a personal narrative that is empowering, self-loving, and reflecting of your value and your authentic self. To bear witness to the pain and narrative of others and offer them a better story that allows them to expand on their abundance and blessings.

JOURNAL QUESTIONS:

What stories about my life am I holding on to?

Do I hold stories reflect who I really am and what I want to create in my life?

What or who do I need to forgive to liberate myself to tell a new story?

What secrets or stories am I holding for others? Do I need to release them?

Write the true story of who I really am....

AFFIRMATION:

The story that I tell myself and the one I tell the world, set the tone and direction for my life. I am the artist and creator of my story. I have the power to rewrite my story every day. The true story I tell from my Heart allows me to serve my Right Place in the Cosmic Plan.

EFT SETUP:

Even though I am afraid to speak my truth, I now share the truth from my heart, and trust that I am safe, and I deeply and completely love and accept myself.

FEBRUARY 8, 2022

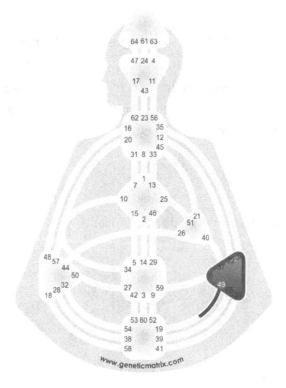

www.geneticmatrix.com

GATE 49: THE CATALYST

CHALLENGE:

To not quit prematurely, failing to start a necessary revolution in your life, to not hold on to unhealthy situations, relationships, or agreements that may compromise your value and worth.

JOURNAL QUESTIONS:

Am I holding on too long?

Is there a circumstance and condition that I am allowing because I am afraid of the emotional energy associated with change?

Do I have a habit of quitting too soon?

Do I fail to do the work associated with creating genuine intimacy?

What do I need to let go of right now to create room for me to align with higher principles?

AFFIRMATION:

I am a cosmic revolutionary. I am aligned with higher principles that support the evolution of humanity. I stand for peace, equity, and sustainability. I align with these principles, and I stand my ground. I do the work to create the intimacy necessary to share my values with others. I value myself and my work enough to only align with relationships that support my vital role.

EFT SETUP:

Even though my emotional response causes me to react/paralyze me, I deeply and completely love and accept myself.

FEBRUARY 13, 2022

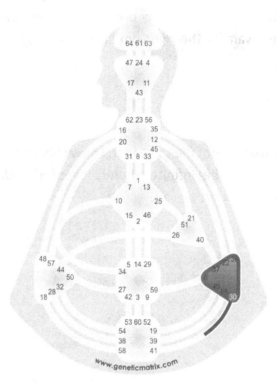

www.geneticmatrix.com

GATE 30: PASSION

CHALLENGE:

To be able to sustain a dream or a vision without burning out. To know which dream to be passionate about. To not let passion overwhelm you and to wait for the right timing to share your passion with the world.

JOURNAL QUESTIONS:

What am I passionate about? Have I lost my passion?

How is my energy? Am I physically burned out? Am I burned out on my idea?

What do I need to do to sustain my vision or dream about what I am inspired to create in my life?

Do I have a dream or vision I am avoiding because I'm afraid it won't come true?

AFFIRMATION:

I am a passionate creator. I use the intensity of my passion to increase my emotional energy and sustain the power of my dream and what I imagine for Life. I trust in the Divine flow, and I wait for the right timing and the right circumstances to act on my dream.

EFT SETUP:

Even though my excitement feels like fear, I now choose to go forward with my passion on fire, fully trusting the infinite abundance of the Universe, and I deeply and completely love and accept myself.

FEBRUARY 16, 2022 – FULL MOON

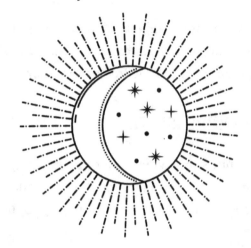

 Leo 27 degrees, 59 minutes

Gate 29 – The Gate of Devotion

Full moon energy invites us to explore what we need to release and let go of in order to stay in alignment with our intentions.

We continue our focus on relationships this month with a Full Moon highlighting the theme of devotion and commitment. This is a powerful time to assess the status of your commitments and what you are devoted to. Sometimes this energy highlights the need to explore what we've said yes to in our lives and to explore if our yes is amplifying our wellbeing or if we are over-committed and co-dependent.

This Full Moon encourages you to explore what you want to commit to. What do you want to say yes to? Is there anything you need to say no to? What do you need to release in your relationships to create room for something more worthy of who you are and what you want to be experiencing? Do you need to make a bolder stand for what you want in order to cultivate more passion and desire in your life?

 CHALLENGE:

To discover what and who you need to devote yourself to. To sustain yourself so that you can sustain your devotion. To learn to say no to what you need to say no to, and to learn to say yes to what you want to say yes to.

OPTIMAL EXPRESSION:

The ability to respond to committing to the right thing. To know that your perseverance and determination changes the narrative of the world and shows people what is possible. Your devotion sets the tone for the direction that life takes you.

UNBALANCED EXPRESSION:

To over-commit. To not know when to let go and when enough is enough. To fail to commit to the right thing. To burn out and deplete yourself because you fail to say yes to yourself. To do something just because you can, not because you want to.

CONTEMPLATIONS:

What devotion do you have right now that drives you? Is this a devotion that inspires you, or do you feel overly obligated to it?

Who would you be and what would you choose if you gave yourself permission to say no more often?

What would you like to say no to that you are saying yes to right now?

What obligations do you need to take off your plate right now?

What would you like to devote yourself to?

AFFIRMATION:

I have an extraordinary ability to devote myself to the manifestation of an idea. My commitment to my story and to the fulfillment of my intention changes the story of what is possible in my own life and for humanity. I choose my commitments with great care. I devote myself to what is vital for the evolution of the world, and I nurture myself first because my wellbeing is the foundation of what I create.

FEBRUARY 19, 2022

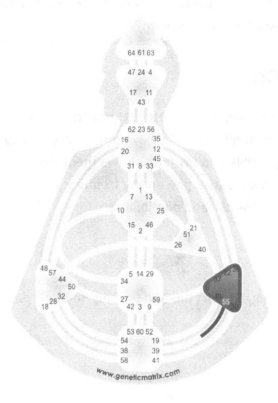

GATE 55: FAITH

CHALLENGE:

To learn to trust Source. To know that you are fully supported To become proficient in the art of emotional alignment *as* your most creative power.

JOURNAL QUESTIONS:

Do I trust that I am fully supported? What do I need to do to deepen that trust?

How can I align myself with abundant emotional energy?

What practices or shifts do I need to make in my life to live and create in a more aligned way?

Do I surround myself with beauty? How can I deepen my experience of beauty in my life?

What do I have faith in now?

What old gods of limitation do I need to stop worshipping?

Go on a miracle hunt. Take stock of everything good that has happened in my life. How much magic have I been blessed with?

AFFIRMATION:

I am perfectly and divinely supported. I know that all my needs and desires are being fulfilled. My trust in my support allows me to create beyond the limitation of what others think is possible and my faith shows them the way. I use my emotional energy as the source of my creative power. My frequency of faith lifts others and opens up a greater world of potential and possibility.

EFT SETUP:

Even though I struggle with faith and trusting Source, I deeply and completely love and accept myself.

FEBRUARY 24, 2022

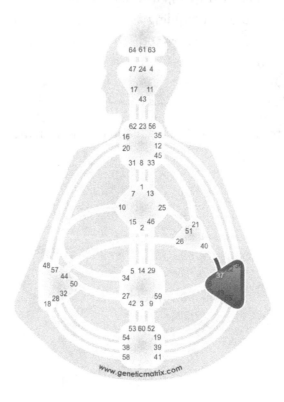

www.geneticmatrix.com

GATE 37: PEACE

CHALLENGE:

To find inner peace as the true source to outer peace. To not let chaos and outer circumstances knock you off your center and disrupt your peace.

JOURNAL QUESTIONS:

What habits, practices and routines do I have that cultivate my inner alignment with sustainable peace?

When I feel that my outer world is chaotic and disrupted how do I cultivate inner peace?

What do I need to do to cultivate a peaceful emotional frequency?

AFFIRMATION:

I am an agent of peace. My being, aligned with peace, creates an energy of contagious peace around me. I practice holding a peaceful frequency of energy, and I respond to the world with an intention of creating sustainable peace.

EFT SETUP:

Even though I struggle to create peace and harmony in my life, I deeply and completely love and accept myself.

MARCH 2, 2022

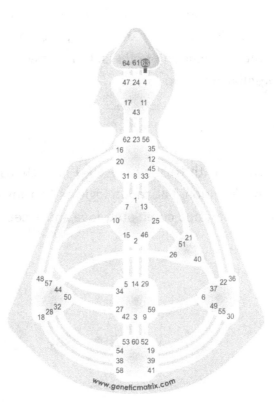

www.geneticmatrix.com

GATE 63: CURIOSITY

CHALLENGE:

To not let self-doubt and suspicion cause you to stop being curious.

JOURNAL QUESTIONS:

Am I curious about life?

Do I regularly allow myself to be curious about what else is possible in the world? In my life?

Do I doubt myself and my ideas?

What needs to happen for me to unlock my need to be right about an idea and to allow myself to dream of possibilities again?

AFFIRMATION:

My curiosity makes me a conduit of possibility thinking. I ask questions that stimulate imaginations. I allow the questions of my mind to seed dreams that stimulate my imagination and the imagination of others. I share my questions as an opening to the fulfillment of potential in the world.

EFT SETUP:

Even though I struggle with trusting myself, I now choose to relax and know that I know. I listen to my intuition. I abandon logic and let my Higher Knowing anchor my spirit in trust, and I deeply and completely love and accept myself.

MARCH 2, 2022 – NEW MOON

 Pisces 12 degrees, 6 minutes

Gate 63 – The Gate of Curiosity

New Moon energy invites us to explore how we can deepen our alignment with our intentions and asks us to focus on what we want to grow and expand on in our lives.

The word for this New Moon cycle is dream. We begin this cycle with the theme of possibility and curiosity, inspiring in us the question, "What else is possible?" We are giving ourselves permission to stretch beyond what we know is possible and to play with possibilities with a large degree of curiosity and wonder.

The other theme highlighted by this New Moon Cycle is gratitude. A lot of us resist gratitude, especially when things aren't going according to our plan. The New Moon encourages us to shift our perspective and to focus on what is working as a foundation for greater growth. The more you appreciate what you have, the better your perspective is for growth and expansion.

We're embarking on a revolution of creativity. The more you are willing to leave behind old limits and engage with the world through the lens of curiosity and wonder, the more you open up your mind to bigger dreams! Dream big!

 CHALLENGE:

To not let self-doubt and suspicion cause you to stop being curious.

OPTIMAL EXPRESSION:

The ability to use questioning and curiosity as a way of stimulating dreams of new possibilities and potentials. Thoughts that inspire the question of what needs to happen to make an idea a reality.

UNBALANCED EXPRESSION:

Doubt (especially self-doubt) that leads to suspicion and the struggle for certainty. The unwillingness to question an old idea. The loss of curiosity.

CONTEMPLATIONS:

Are you curious about life?

Do you regularly allow yourself to be curious about what else is possible in the world? In your life?

Do you doubt yourself and your ideas?

What needs to happen for you to unlock your need to be right about an idea and to allow yourself to dream of possibilities again?

AFFIRMATION:

My curiosity makes me a conduit of possibility thinking. I ask questions that stimulate imaginations. I allow the questions of my mind to seed dreams that stimulate my imagination and the imagination of others. I share my questions as an opening to the fulfillment of potential in the world.

MARCH 8, 2022

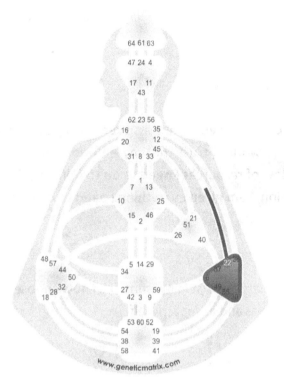

www.geneticmatrix.com

GATE 22: SURRENDER

CHALLENGE:

To trust that your passions and deepest desires are supported by the Universal flow of abundance. To have the courage to follow your passion and know that you will be supported. To learn to regulate your emotional energy so that you have faith that everything will unfold perfectly.

JOURNAL QUESTIONS:

Where am I denying my passion in my life? Where have I settled for less than what I want because I'm afraid I can't get what I want?

What do I need to do to fully activate my passion? What is one bold step towards my genius that I could take right now?

Do I trust the Universe?

What do I need to do to deepen my trust?

Do I have a regular practice that supports me in sustaining a high frequency of emotional energy and alignment?

What needs to be healed, released, aligned, and brought to my awareness for me to deepen my faith?

AFFIRMATION:

I am a global change agent. I am inspired with passions that serve the purpose of transforming the world. I trust that my emotions and my passion will align me with faith and the flow of resources I need to do to fulfill my life purpose. When I let go and follow my passion, I am given everything I need to change the world.

EFT SETUP:

Even though it is hard to trust in my support, I now choose to trust anyway, and I deeply and completely love and accept myself.

MARCH 13, 2022

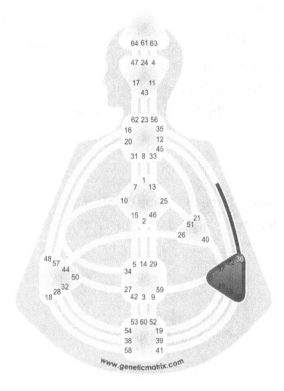

GATE 36: EXPLORATION

CHALLENGE:

To not let boredom cause you to leap into chaos. To learn to stick with something long enough to become skillful and to bear the fruits of your experience.

JOURNAL QUESTIONS:

How does boredom impact my life?

What do I do when I feel bored?

What can I do to keep myself aligned even when I'm bored?

What stories have I experienced that have shattered old patterns and expectations?

How have my stories changed or inspired others?

What do I do to maintain or sustain emotional alignment?

What do I need to add to my daily practice to amp up my emotional energy around my intentions?

AFFIRMATION:

My experiences and stories break old patterns and push the boundaries of the edge of what is possible for humanity. I defy the patterns and I create miracles through my emotional alignment with possibility. I hold my vision and maintain my emotional energy as I wait to bear the fruit of my intentions and my visions.

EFT SETUP:

Even though it is scary to be out of my comfort zone, I now choose to push myself into something new and more aligned with my Truth, and I deeply and completely love and accept myself.

MARCH 18, 2022 – FULL MOON

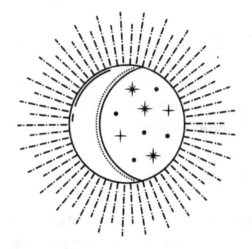

 Virgo 27 degrees, 39 minutes

Gate 6 – The Gate of Impact

Full moon energy invites us to explore what we need to release and let go of in order to stay in alignment with our intentions.

This full moon brings us amazing energy that helps us to remember that not only is dreaming an essential part of the creative process, but also a reminder that we need to dream big enough in order to truly call in the experience and circumstances that match our value and values.

This Full Moon asks you to release and let go of anything that might be keeping you from taking big leaps of faith and moving strongly into a more aligned, abundant, and authentic life.

This is a good time to review the previous New Moon and explore what you need to heal, release, align, or bring into your awareness in order for you to let go of anything that is holding you back from taking bold steps forward towards your dreams.

 ## CHALLENGE:

To become proficient in using emotional energy and learn to trust that your impact is in service to the world. When you understand that your life is a vehicle for service and your energy is being used to influence and impact those around you, you assume greater obligation and responsibility to maintaining a high frequency of energy. The quality of the emotional energy you cultivate influences others to come together in an equitable, sustainable, and peaceful way. Learning to trust that your words and impact will have effect when the timing is correct and to avoid overriding Divine Timing.

OPTIMAL EXPRESSION:

Maintaining a high frequency of emotional energy that supports equitability, sustainability, and peace. Using your emotional alignment to influence others and to serve as an energetic beacon of peace.

UNBALANCED EXPRESSION:

Feeling desperate, emotionally reactive, lacking, and invisible, and being willing to do whatever it takes to use resources and energy for your own good, regardless of the means. Fear that you will never be seen or heard.

CONTEMPLATIONS:

What do you need to do to deepen your trust in Divine Timing?

What do you need to do to prepare yourself to be seen and to have influence?

What do you need to do to sustain your emotional energy in order to align with peaceful and sustainable solutions?

How do you feel about lack? How do you feel about abundance?

How can you create a greater degree of emotional abundance in your life? In your daily practice?

AFFIRMATION:

My emotional energy influences the world around me. I am rooted in the energy of equity, sustainability, and peace. When I am aligned with abundance, I am an energetic source of influence that facilitates elegant solutions to creating peace and wellbeing. I am deliberate and aligned with values that create peace in my life, in my community and in the world.

MARCH 19, 2022

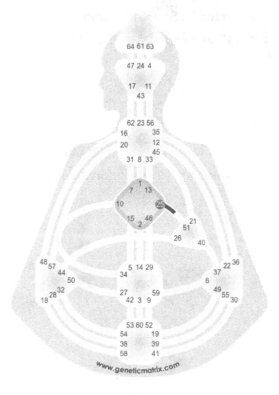

www.geneticmatrix.com

GATE 25: SPIRIT

CHALLENGE:

To trust the Divine Order in all of your life. To learn to connect with Source as the path to creating wellbeing in your life. To remember that your life serves an irreplaceable role in the cosmic plan and to honor that role and to live from it. To trust Source.

JOURNAL QUESTIONS:

Do I trust Source?

Do I have a regular practice that connects me to Source?

Do I know my Life Purpose? Am I living true to my Purpose?

How can I deepen my connection to my Purpose?

AFFIRMATION:

I am an agent of the Divine. My life is the fulfillment of Divine Order and the Cosmic Plan. When I am connected to Source, I serve my right place. I take up no more than my space and no less than my place in the world. I serve and through serving, I am supported.

EFT SETUP:

Even though in the past, I was afraid to follow my heart, I now choose to do what is right for me and know that I am fully supported, and I deeply and completely love and accept myself.

MARCH 25, 2022

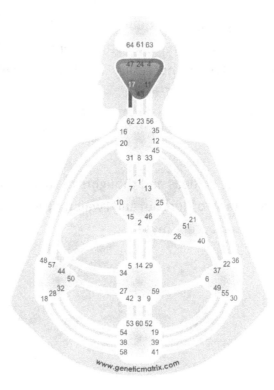

GATE 17: ANTICIPATION

CHALLENGE:

To learn to share your thoughts about possibilities only when people ask for them. To not let doubt and suspicion keep you from seeing the potential of positive outcomes.

JOURNAL QUESTIONS:

What do I need to do to manage my insights and ideas so that they increase the options and potential of others?

How do I feel about holding back from sharing my insights until the timing is right?

What can I do to manage my need to share without waiting for the right timing?

What routines and strategies do I need to cultivate to keep my perspectives expanding and possibility oriented?

How can I improve my ability to manage doubt and fear?

AFFIRMATION:

I use the power of my mind to explore possibilities and potential. I know that the inspirations and insights that I have create exploration and experimentation that can inspire the elegant solutions necessary to skillfully control the challenges facing humanity.

EFT SETUP:

Even though I have a lot of ideas and thoughts to share, I trust that the insights I have to offer are too important to blurt out and I wait for the right people to ask, and I deeply and completely love and accept myself.

MARCH 30, 2022

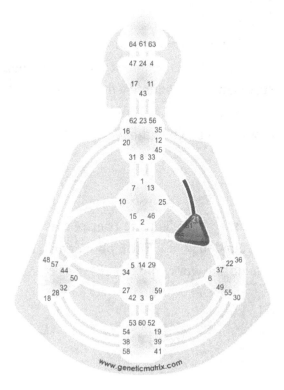

GATE 21: SELF-REGULATION

CHALLENGE:

To learn to let go. To become proficient at self-regulation. To release the need to control others and circumstances. To trust in the Divine and to know that you are supported. Knowing that you are worthy of support, and you don't have to over-compensate.

JOURNAL QUESTIONS:

Where do I need to release control in my life?

Do I trust the Universe?

Do I value myself? Do I trust that I will be supported in accordance with my value?

What do I need to do to create an internal and external environment of self- generosity?

What needs to be healed, released, aligned, and brought to my awareness for me to embrace my true value?

AFFIRMATION:

I am worthy of claiming, protecting, and defending my rightful place in the world. I create an inner and outer environment that is self-generous, and I regulate my environment to sustain a high frequency of alignment with my true value. I know that I am an irreplaceable and precious part of the cosmic plan and I create my life to reflect the importance of my right place in the world.

EFT SETUP:

Even though in the past I felt like I had to control everything, I now surrender to Source and know that my abundance, my TRUE abundance, is available to me when I let go and let the Universe do the work, and I deeply and completely love and accept myself.

APRIL 1, 2022 – NEW MOON

 Aries 11 degrees, 30 minutes

Gate 21 – The Gate of Self-Regulation

New Moon energy invites us to explore how we can deepen our alignment with our intentions and asks us to focus on what we want to grow and expand on in our lives.

This particular New Moon brings us powerful energy for new beginnings that involves establishing new habits and patterns. We are invited to explore the strength of our self-worth and to cultivate habits that regulate the inner and outer environment.

This is a vital time to explore your inner self-talk and to reflect on your personal narrative and how it impacts how much good you are allowing into your life. What intentions do you need to set in order for you to allow yourself to experience more?

It is also a time to set new habits with how you manage your outer environment. Are you creating a world for yourself that reflects your true value? Are your habits and patterns supporting your sustainability and your value?

 ## CHALLENGE:

To learn to let go. To become proficient at self-regulation. To release the need to control others and circumstances. To trust in the Divine and to know that you are supported. Knowing that you are worthy of support, and you don't have to overcompensate.

OPTIMAL EXPRESSION:

The ability to regulate your inner and outer environment in order to sustain a vibrational frequency that reflects your true value. The ability to be self-generous and to set boundaries that maintain your value and support you in being sustainable in the world. To take the actions necessary to honor your unique role in the cosmic plan.

UNBALANCED EXPRESSION:

To feel the need to control life, others, resources, etc. out of fear that you are not worthy of being supported.

CONTEMPLATIONS:

Where do you need to release control in your life?

Do you trust the Universe?

Do you value yourself?

Do you trust that you will be supported in accordance with your value?

What do you need to do to create an internal and external environment of self-generosity?

What needs to be healed, released, aligned, and brought to your awareness for you to embrace your true value?

AFFIRMATION:

I am worthy of claiming, protecting, and defending my right place in the world. I create an inner and outer environment that is self-generous, and I regulate my environment to sustain a high frequency of alignment with my true value. I know that I am an irreplaceable and precious part of the cosmic plan, and I create my life to reflect the importance of my right place in the world.

APRIL 5, 2022

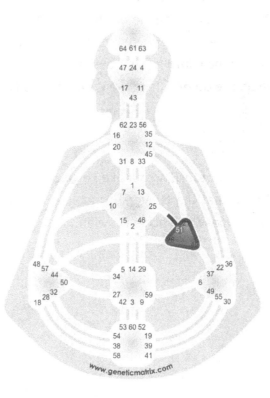

GATE 51: INITIATION

CHALLENGE:

To not let the unexpected cause you to lose your faith. To not let a pattern of unexpected events cause you to lose your connection with your purpose and Source. To learn to use the power of your own story of initiation to initiate others into fulfilling their rightful place in the Cosmic Plan.

JOURNAL QUESTIONS:

What has shock and the unexpected taught me in my life?

How can I deepen my connection to Source?

How can my experiences of initiation be shared with others? What am I here to wake people up to?

AFFIRMATION:

I navigate change and transformation with Grace. I know that when my life takes a twist or a turn, it is my soul calling me out to serve at a higher level. I use disruption as a catalyst for my own growth and expansion. I am a teacher and an initiator. I use my ability to transform pain into growth and power to help others navigate through crisis and emerge on the other side of crisis empowered and aligned.

EFT SETUP:

Even though things are not turning out like I expected, I now choose to embrace the unexpected and trust that the Universe is always serving my Greater Good, and I deeply and completely love and accept myself.

APRIL 11, 2022

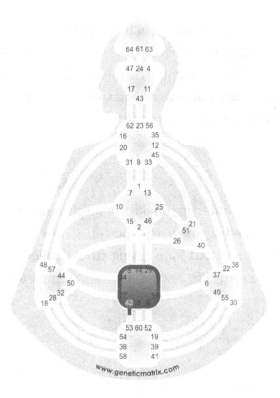

www.geneticmatrix.com

GATE 42: CONCLUSION

CHALLENGE:

To learn to bring things to completion. To allow yourself to be led to where you need to be to finish things. To value your ability to know how to finish and to learn to give up your need to try to start everything. To finish things in order to create space for something new.

JOURNAL QUESTIONS:

Do I own and value my natural gift of knowing how to bring things to completion?

What things in my life do I need to finish in order to make room for something new?

Am I holding on to old circumstances and patterns because I'm afraid to let them go?

Do I judge myself for not starting things?

How can I learn to be gentler with myself?

AFFIRMATION:

I am gifted at knowing when and how to finish things. I respond to bringing events, experiences, and relationships to a conclusion in order to create space for something new and more abundant. I can untangle the cosmic entanglements that keep people stuck in old patterns. My ability to re-align and complete things helps others create space for transformation and expansion.

EFT SETUP:

Even though I have hesitated in the past to finish what I needed to finish in order to make room for something new and better, I now choose to bring things to a powerful ending. I know that I am taking strong action to create space for what I truly want to create in my life, and I deeply and completely love myself.

APRIL 16, 2022

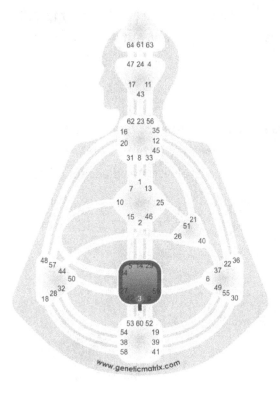

www.geneticmatrix.com

GATE 3: INNOVATION

CHALLENGE:

To learn to trust in Divine Timing and to know that your ideas and insights will be transmitted to the world when the world is ready.

JOURNAL QUESTIONS:

Where has Divine Timing worked out in my life? What has waiting taught me?

Do I trust in Divine Timing?

If the opportunity to share my ideas with the world presented itself today, would I be ready?

If I am not ready, what do I need to prepare to be ready?

AFFIRMATION:

I am here to bring change to the world. My natural ability to see what else is possible to create something new is my strength and my gift. I patiently cultivate my inspiration and use my understanding of what is needed to help evolve the world.

EFT SETUP:

Even though it is scary to take the first step, I now trust the Universe and my ability to be innovative and know that I stand on the cusp of the fulfillment of my Big Dreams. I deeply and completely love and accept myself.

APRIL 16, 2022 – FULL MOON

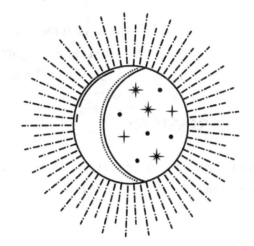

 Libra 26 degrees, 45 minutes
Gate 50 – The Gate of Nurturing

Full moon energy invites us to explore what we need to release and let go of in order to stay in alignment with our intentions.

This Full Moon cycle brings us a deep exploration of our willingness to suspend doubt in order to cultivate deeper faith. We are being brought face-to-face with the question of what doubts we need to release in order for us to create beyond the limitations of what we think is possible.

We are also being invited to explore the nature of our relationships and whether our partnership agreements are aligned with our value and our values, and whether our partnerships are enhancing our well-being and evolution or keeping us locked in old patterns that need to be released and re-negotiated.

 CHALLENGE:

To learn to nurture in an empowering way. To not deplete yourself in the name of nurturing others. To not let your fear of letting other people down (or suffering the consequences of their own actions) cause you to overcompensate or feel guilty.

OPTIMAL EXPRESSION:

The ability to nurture yourself so that you have more to give others. The intuition to know what others need to bring them into greater alignment with Love. To teach and share what you have to increase the wellbeing of others.

UNBALANCED EXPRESSION:

To over-nurture to the point of burnout. To care to the point of overtaking. To let guilt cause you to make commitments that don't feel good or aligned.

CONTEMPLATIONS:

What new rules do I need to play by? Do I need to create new rules in my relationships, my business, for my health, wealth, and welfare?

Do I love myself? Do I need to nurture myself more? Do I have the strength and foundation to love freely? Do I feel safe in love?

AFFIRMATION:

I establish the rules for my reality. I take care and nourish myself so that I may take care and nourish others. Everything I do for others I do for myself first in order to sustain my energy and power. I rule with self-love and then love freely.

APRIL 22, 2022

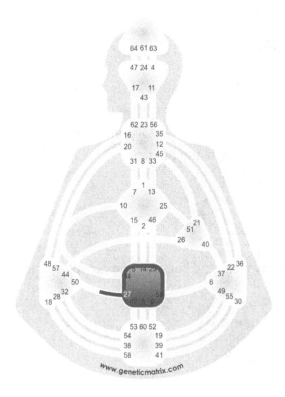

GATE 27: ACCOUNTABILITY

CHALLENGE:

To care without over-caring. To allow others to assume responsibility for their own challenges and choices. To learn to accept other people's values. To not let guilt cause you to compromise what is good and right for you.

JOURNAL QUESTIONS:

Am I taking responsibility for things that aren't mine to be responsible for? Whose problem is it?

Can I return the responsibility for the problem back to its rightful owner?

What role does guilt play in motivating me?

Can I let go of the guilt?

What different choices might I make if I didn't feel guilty?

What obligations do I need to set down in order for me to take better care of myself?

Are there places where I need to soften my judgements of other people's values?

AFFIRMATION:

I have a nurturing and loving nature. It is my gift to be able to love and care for others. I know that the greatest expression of my love is to treat others as capable and powerful. I support when necessary, and I let go with love so my loved ones can discover their own strength and power.

EFT SETUP:

Even though it is hard to say no, I now choose to take the actions that are correct for me. I release my guilt, and I deeply and completely love and accept myself.

APRIL 28, 2022

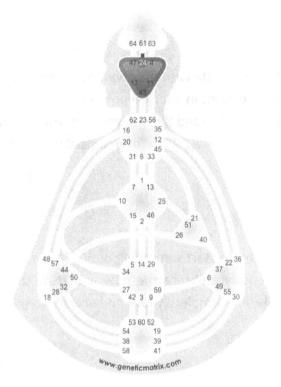

www.geneticmatrix.com

GATE 24: BLESSINGS

CHALLENGE:

To learn to allow what you truly deserve in your life. To not rationalize an experience that allowed for less than you deserve. To find the blessings and power from painful experiences and to use them as catalysts for transformation.

JOURNAL QUESTIONS:

What are the blessings I learned from my greatest painful experiences?

Can I see how these experiences served to teach me?

What did I learn?

What am I grateful for from the past?

Where might I be rationalizing staying stuck or settling for less than what I really want or deserve?

What do I need to do to break out of this pattern?

AFFIRMATION:

I embrace the Mystery of Life with the awareness that the infinite generosity of the Universe gives me blessings in every event in my life. I find the blessings from the pain. I grow and expand beyond the limitations of my experiences and stories. I use what I have learned to create a life and circumstances that reflect the miracle that I am.

EFT SETUP:

Even though it is scary to start something new... I am afraid I am not ready... I now choose to courageously embrace the new and trust that everything is in Divine Order, and I deeply and completely love and accept myself.

APRIL 30, 2022
NEW MOON AND PARTIAL SOLAR ECLIPSE

Taurus 10 degrees, 35 minutes – New Moon

Taurus 10 degrees, 27 minutes – Eclipse

Gate 24 – The Gate of Blessings

New Moon energy invites us to explore how we can deepen our alignment with our intentions and asks us to focus on what we want to grow and expand on in our lives.

Eclipse energy amplifies the intensity of the New Moon.

The New Moon and Eclipse power-combo brings us an amplified energy for new beginnings and new intention. The highlighted theme with this celestial combo encourages us to explore our personal narrative and invites us to look at where we may have settled for less than what we want or deserve.

This energy gives us perspective on the past and allows us to shift our focus away from the question of why something has happened to us and towards the exploration of how an event might have happened to help us grow and evolve. This is not about condoning any pain or trauma that may have happened in the past, but about reclaiming power over old narratives so that you no longer define yourself as a victim.

With this amplified energy for starting anew, we are encouraged to create a new narrative about what we truly deserve and reminds us to never settle for less than what we want and what we're worthy of receiving.

CHALLENGE:

To learn to find the blessings in all situations, even the painful ones. To learn to use painful circumstances as a way to grow in your own power and sense of value. To learn to value yourself enough to not rationalize settling for less than what you deserve.

OPTIMAL EXPRESSION:

To recognize all experiences have the potential for growth and expansion. To redefine the stories of your experiences to reflect what you learned and how you grew. To be grateful for all of your life experiences and to liberate yourself from stories that no longer serve you.

UNBALANCED EXPRESSION:

To rationalize staying stuck in victimhood or staying in old stuck patterns of behavior that don't support the highest expression of your value.

CONTEMPLATIONS:

Make a list of everything that feels good and is working in your life.

What have your greatest challenges taught you?

Where might you be settling for less than what you want or deserve?

AFFIRMATION:

I give my attention to my progress and all that is good. I focus on what is working, what is aligning, and I trust that all that is good will grow. I celebrate my successes and focus on creating more success by simply attending to that which is correct for me.

MAY 4, 2022

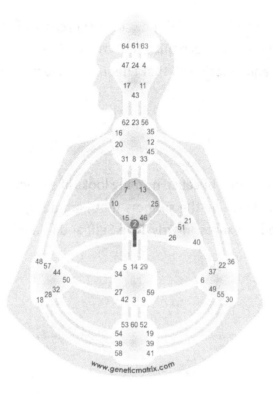

www.geneticmatrix.com

GATE 2: ALLOWING

CHALLENGE:

To love yourself enough to open to the flow of support, love, and abundance. To incrementally increase over the course of your life what you're willing to allow yourself to receive. To learn to know that you are valuable and lovable simply because you exist.

JOURNAL QUESTIONS:

Do I ask for help when I need it? Why or why not?

Do I trust the Universe/God/Spirit/Source to support me in fulfilling my intentions?

Am I grateful for what I have? Make a list of everything I'm grateful for.

Can I transform my worry into trust?

Do I believe that I deserve to be supported?

AFFIRMATION:

I allow myself to receive the full flow of resources and abundance I need to fully express all of who I am. I recognize that my life is a vital, irreplaceable part of the cosmic tapestry and I receive all that I need because it helps me contribute all that I am.

EFT SETUP:

Even though I am scared because nothing looks like I thought it would, I now choose to relax, trust, and receive the support that I am designed to receive. I know that I will be supported in expressing my True Self, and I deeply and completely love and accept myself.

MAY 10, 2022

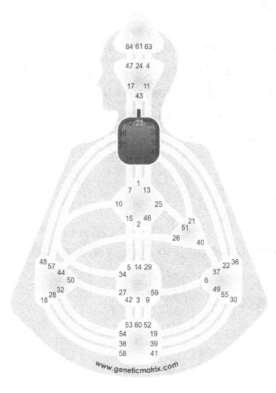

www.geneticmatrix.com

GATE 23: TRANSMISSION

CHALLENGE:

To recognize that change and transformation are inevitable. To know what needs to happen next, to wait for the right timing and the right people to share your insights with. To not jump the gun and try to convince people to understand what you know. To not let yourself slip into negativity and despair when people aren't ready.

JOURNAL QUESTIONS:

How can I strengthen my connection to Source?

Do I trust what I know?

What comes up for me when I know something, but I don't know how I know what I know?

How do I handle myself when I know something but the people around me aren't ready to hear it yet?

AFFIRMATION:

I change the world with what I know. My insights and awarenesses have the ability to transform the way people think and perceive the world. I know that my words are powerful and transformative. I trust that the people who are ready for the change that I bring will ask me for what I know. I am a vessel for my knowingness, and I nurture myself while I wait to share what I know.

EFT SETUP:

Even though in the past I shut down my voice, I now speak my truth and offer the contribution of my unique spirit to the world, and I deeply and completely love and accept myself.

MAY 15, 2022

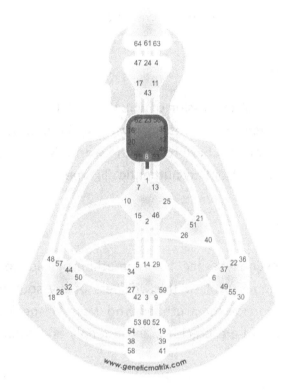

GATE 8: FULFILLMENT

CHALLENGE:

To learn to express yourself authentically. To wait for the right people to see the value of who you are and to share yourself with them, with vulnerability and through all of your heart. To learn to trust that you are a unique expression of the Divine with a purpose and a path. To find that path and to walk it without self-judgment or holding back.

JOURNAL QUESTIONS:

Do I feel safe being vulnerable?

What experiences have caused me to feel unsafe expressing my true self? Can I rewrite those stories?

What would an uncompromising life look like for me?

What do I need to remove from my current life to make my life more authentic?

What is one bold action I can take right now that would allow me to express who I am more authentically in the world?

What is my true passion? What do I dream of?

AFFIRMATION:

I am devoted to the full expression of who I am. I defend and protect the story of my Life. I know that when I am expressing myself, without hesitation or limitation, I AM the contribution that I am here to give the world. Being myself IS my life purpose and my direction flows from my authentic alignment.

EFT SETUP:

Even though I question whether I have something of value to add to the world, I now choose to courageously follow the whispers of my soul and live a life that is a powerful expression of the truth of who I am. I speak my truth. I value my contribution. I know I am precious, and I deeply and completely love and accept myself.

MAY 16, 2022
FULL MOON AND LUNAR ECLIPSE

Scorpio 25 degrees, 16 minutes – Full Moon

Scorpio 25 degrees, 17 minutes – Eclipse

Gate 14 – The Gate of Creation

Full moon energy invites us to explore what we need to release and let go of in order to stay in alignment with our intentions. Eclipse energy amplifies the intensity of the Full Moon.

Today's Full Moon and Lunar Eclipse combo gives us a power-packed energy burst to help us burn away our limitations and amplify our alignment with our forward momentum. With the Full Moon shining on the Gate 14, we are exploring anything that is keeping us from stepping into the full experience of our abundance and true creative essence.

This Full Moon cycle invites us to explore better and more aligned ways to tap into our natural support and to not compromise who we are or what we long to share with the world. We are deepening our connection to our purpose and our authentic self-expression, discovering that we are truly supported and abundant when we are unwavering and relentless in fully expressing our Authentic Self.

CHALLENGE:

To learn to make peace with money. To learn to trust that you will always have opportunities. To learn to trust in sufficiency.

OPTIMAL EXPRESSION:

The ability to be at peace about having resources. To be in a constant state of trust that everything you need will show up in your outer reality in accordance with your alignment with Source. The resources you have allow you to increase the resources for others. To change the definition of work. To no longer work for material gain but work for the sake of transforming the world and being in the flow of life. To know that support flows from alignment with your Heart.

UNBALANCED EXPRESSION:

To panic about work and money. To overwork or to accept work that you don't want simply for the sake of material gain.

CONTEMPLATIONS:

Make a list of everything you are doing right now that you find inspiring and delicious. Make a commitment to yourself to follow at least one of these inspirations each day.

What would your life look like if you only followed your passion? What would you be doing? What would your life feel like? What would be your energy level?

Do you trust the Universe to support you in following your bliss? Is it okay to make money doing what you love? Can you do what you love and know that you will be supported?

AFFIRMATION:

I respond to the things which bring me joy. I pay attention to my excitement and passion and allow myself to trust that the Universe is deliciously conspiring to find ways to support me in the pursuit of my passion. I do what I want to do. I do what feels correct. I honor my joy and excitement and commit to feeling good, knowing that this is the most important contribution I can make to the planet at this time.

MAY 21, 2022

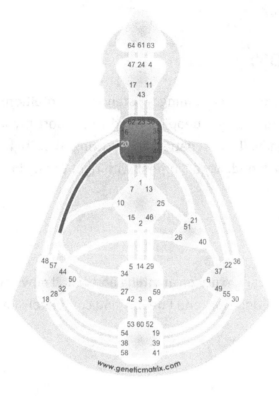

www.geneticmatrix.com

GATE 20: PATIENCE

CHALLENGE:

To be patient and control the ability to wait. To be prepared and watchful but resist the urge to act if the timing isn't right or if there are details that still need to be readied.

JOURNAL QUESTIONS:

How do I manage my need for action?

Am I patient?

Do I trust in Divine Timing?

Do I trust my intuition?

What needs to be healed, released, aligned, and brought to my awareness for me to trust my intuition?

What needs to be healed, released, aligned, and brought to my awareness for me to trust my intuition?

AFFIRMATION:

I am in the flow of perfect timing. I listen to my intuition. I prepare. I gather the experience, resources, and people I need to support my ideas and my principles. When I am ready, I wait patiently, knowing that right timing is the key to transforming the world. My alignment with right timing increases my influence and my power.

EFT SETUP:

Even though it is scary to not *do* anything and wait, I now choose to trust the infinite abundance of the Universe, and I deeply and completely love and accept myself.

MAY 27, 2022

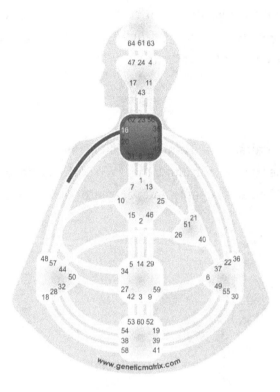

GATE 16: ZEST

CHALLENGE:

To learn to temper your enthusiasm by making sure you are prepared enough for whatever it is you are trying to do or create.

JOURNAL QUESTIONS:

Do I trust my gut?

Do I need to slow down and make sure I've done my homework before I take action?

Have I sidelined my enthusiasm because other people have told me that I cannot do what I am dreaming of doing?

AFFIRMATION:

I am a faith-filled contagious force. I take guided actions and I trust my intuition and awareness to let me know when I am prepared and ready to leap into expanding my experience and genius. My enthusiasm inspires others to trust in themselves and to take their own giant leaps of growth.

EFT SETUP:

Even though I am afraid that I am not fulfilling my life purpose and I am wasting my life, I now choose to relax and know that I am in the perfect place at the perfect time to fulfill my destiny, and I deeply and completely love and accept myself.

MAY 30, 2022 – NEW MOON

 Gemini 9 degrees, 3 minutes
Gate 16 – The Gate of Zest

New Moon energy invites us to explore how we can deepen our alignment with our intentions and asks us to focus on what we want to grow and expand on in our lives.

This is the giddiest of New Moons, full of sparkly energy for enthusiastic new beginnings. We've been clearing out the old layers of doubt and limitation these past few months. Now it is time to zestfully take the first step in our new journey of expansion.

But, there's a catch…

This New Moon demands that we do our homework, that we focus and make sure that our zesty enthusiasm is rooted in a foundation of knowledge and experience. We will arrive at our destination unscathed if we focus, take care of the necessary details, and make sure that we've double-checked all the facts so that we're ready to launch.

Our preparation pays off and we are poised to reap the rewards of all the hard work.

 CHALLENGE:

To learn to prepare when it is necessary and to assess whether you are genuinely ready before your enthusiasm overrides your need to build a solid foundation first.

OPTIMAL EXPRESSION:

The courage to leap into action and to inspire others to act, even if you don't know all the details. The courage to trust your own intuition that the timing is right, and you are ready enough even if you don't know exactly how your journey will unfold. Faith in the outcome.

UNBALANCED EXPRESSION:

Failing to do your homework before you leap into action, sometimes causing you to scramble or to have to face the chaotic results of your leaping before you look. Quitting before trying because the fear of making a mistake is too strong.

CONTEMPLATIONS:

What dreams are beginning to come to fruition? What is your experimentation teaching you? What are you needing to tweak?

What beliefs may be part of creating the manifestation of your experiments? Are there any old beliefs that you need to release?

Can you imagine the full enthusiastic expression of your unique gifts and talents?

AFFIRMATION:

I allow myself to create and experiment. Experimentation and exploration are a natural part of my creative self and allows me to find the correct pattern for the expression of my talents and my soul's journey. It is in the relentless pursuit of this journey that I live my joy.

JUNE 2, 2022

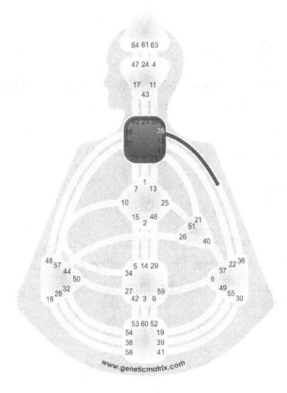

GATE 35: EXPERIENCE

CHALLENGE:

To not let experience lead to feeling jaded or bored. To have the courage to share what you know from your experience. To know which experiences are worth participating in. To let your natural ability to become accomplished at anything keep you from being enthusiastic about learning something new. To embrace that even though you know how to know, you don't know everything.

JOURNAL QUESTIONS:

Where am I finding passion in my life?

Do I need to create or discover more passion in my life right now?

Do I share my knowledge and the stories of my experiences?

Do I see the value of what I have to share?

What am I curious about?

How can I expand on that curiosity?

 ## AFFIRMATION:

I am an experienced, wise, and knowledgeable resource for others. My experiences in life have added to the rich tapestry that is the story of Humanity. I share my stories with others because my experiences open doorways of possibility for others. My stories help others create miracles in their lives.

 ## EFT SETUP:

Even though in the past I struggled to stay focused and move forward, I now trust myself to take the next steps on manifesting my dream. I am focused, clear, and moving forward, and I deeply and completely love and accept myself.

JUNE 8, 2022

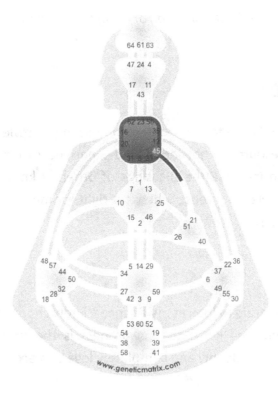

GATE 45: DISTRIBUTION

CHALLENGE:

To share and use your resources for the greater good of the whole. To learn to manage resources judiciously so that they benefit the greatest number of people. To teach as a pathway of sharing.

JOURNAL QUESTIONS:

Do I like to share?

What do I have to give the world?

How do I own my right leadership?

Am I comfortable as a leader?

Do I shrink from leadership?

Do I overcompensate by pushing too hard with my leadership?

Do I trust that when the right people are ready, I will be pressed into action as a leader and a teacher?

What do I need to heal, release, align or bring to my awareness to trust my leadership energy more?

AFFIRMATION:

I am a teacher and a leader. I use my resources, my knowledge, and my experience to expand the resources, knowledge, and experiences of others. I use my blessings of abundance to increase the blessings of others. I know that I am a vehicle of wisdom and knowledge. I sense when it is right for me to share who I am and what I know with others.

EFT SETUP:

Even though I'm afraid to look at my finances, I now choose to take a real look at my financial numbers and know that awareness is the first step to increasing my financial status, and I deeply and completely love and accept myself.

JUNE 14, 2022

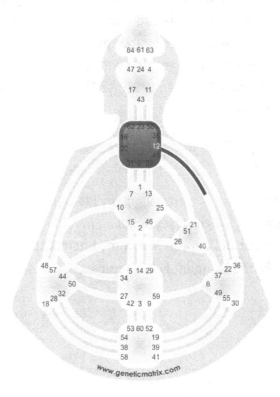

www.geneticmatrix.com

GATE 12: THE CHANNEL

CHALLENGE:

To honor the self enough to wait for the right time and *mood* to speak. To know that *shyness* is actually a signal that the timing is not right to share transformational insights and expressions. When the timing IS right, to have the courage to share what you feel and sense. To honor the fact that your voice and the words you offer are a direct connection to Source and you channel the potential for transformation. To own your creative power.

JOURNAL QUESTIONS:

How has shyness caused me to judge myself?

What do I need to do to cultivate a deeper connection with Source?

What do I need to do to connect more deeply with my creative power?

AFFIRMATION:

I am a creative being. My words, my self-expression, my creative offerings have the power to change the way people see and understand the world. I am a vessel of Divine Transformation and I serve Source through the words that I share. I wait for the right timing, and when I am aligned with timing and flow, my creativity creates beauty and Grace in the world. I am a Divine Channel, and I trust that the words that I serve will open the Hearts of others.

EFT SETUP:

Even though I am afraid that I am failing my life purpose and mission, I now choose to know that I am in the right place fulfilling my right purpose. All I need to do is to follow my strategy, be deliberate, follow my heart, and all will be exactly as it needs to be, and I deeply and completely love and accept myself.

JUNE 14, 2022 – SUPER FULL MOON

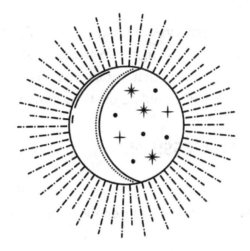

 Sagittarius 23 degrees, 24 minutes
Gate 11 – The Gate of the Conceptualist

Full moon energy invites us to explore what we need to release and let go of in order to stay in alignment with our intentions.

This Full Moon brings with it an abundance of ideas, but also the need to wait for right timing to implement them. We are deeply conditioned to think that we have to make all of our ideas come true and that our hard work and will helps to manifest them.

The reality of the situation is that inspiration is one thing. Implementation and the timing for implementation is another. We must learn to be patient, to wait and trust that when the timing is right, we will get some kind of confirmation that it is time to initiate and implement our ideas.

This Full Moon encourages us to explore the quality of our relationship with abundance and Source and challenges us to release anything that is keeping us from relaxing into Right Timing.

 CHALLENGE:

To learn how to hold on to ideas until the time is right to either share them or implement them. To learn that not all of your ideas should be implemented. To use the power of your creative thinking to inspire others.

OPTIMAL EXPRESSION:

The awareness that you are a vessel for ideas. To understand that those ideas are for you to hold and protect until the right person comes along for you to share them with. To relax as the vessel and know that not all ideas are yours to build upon. To use the power of your inspiration to stimulate the imagination of yourself and others.

UNBALANCED EXPRESSION:

To feel pressured and anxious in your attempt to take action on all of your ideas resulting in a series of scattered and frenetic efforts that leave you feeling unfulfilled and frustrated.

CONTEMPLATIONS:

Evaluate your achievements and accomplishments of the last few weeks. What ideas do you have to improve what you've done? What did you learn?

Keep a running list of ideas this week. You never know when you might find the right person to share them with or when you may hit upon the million-dollar idea for your life!

***Remember, the 11 is the Gate of Ideas. You don't have to manifest all of them... or any of them. If an idea is correct for you, it will show up in your life correctly, according to your personal Human Design strategy.

AFFIRMATION:

I honor my inner creative process. I am grateful for every lesson and adventure I have in life, and I know that each story of my life experience adds beautiful, rich threads to the tapestry of my own Life Story and the Story of Humanity. I relax and enjoy the quest for Truth in my life, knowing that the more I learn, the more I grow and that the learning and growing never stops. I allow myself to savor every moment and serve as the creative vessel I am. I relax, breathe, trust, and let the ideas flow!

JUNE 20, 2022

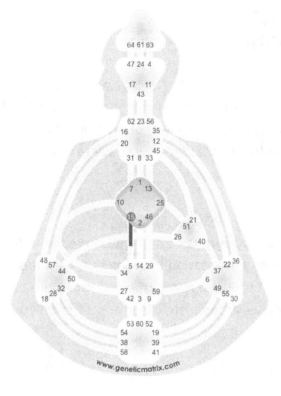

z

GATE 15: COMPASSION

CHALLENGE:

To learn to allow yourself to be in the flow of your own rhythm. To not beat yourself up because you don't have daily **habits**. To have the courage to do the right thing even if you are worried about not having enough. To share from the Heart without giving up your Heart and serving as a **martyr**.

JOURNAL QUESTIONS:

Do I trust my own rhythm?

Do I share from the Heart?

Do I over share?

Does my sharing compromise my own Heart?

Do I judge my own rhythm?

Can I find peace in aligning with my own rhythm?

What old patterns do I need to break?

AFFIRMATION:

Like the power of a hurricane to transform the shoreline, my unique rhythm brings change to the landscape of my life and the world around me. I embrace my own rhythm and acknowledge the power of my own Heart. I share with ease, and I serve my own Heart as the foundation of all I have to give the world.

EFT SETUP:

Even though I feel powerless to make a difference in the world, I now choose to follow my heart and my passion knowing that I am the greatest gift I can give the world. The more I show up as my true self, the more I empower others to do the same, and I deeply and completely love and accept myself.

JUNE 25, 2022

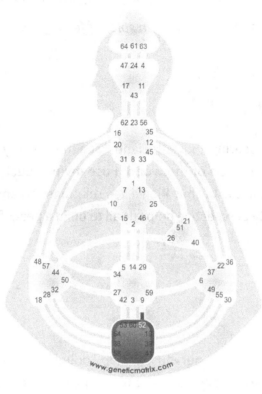

www.geneticmatrix.com

GATE 52: PERSPECTIVE

CHALLENGE:

To learn to stay focused even when you're overwhelmed by a bigger perspective. To see the big picture, to not let the massive nature of what you know confuse you and cause you to struggle with where to put your energy and attention.

JOURNAL QUESTIONS:

What do I do to maintain and sustain my focus?

Is there anything in my environment or my life that I need to move out of the way in order for me to deepen my focus?

How do I manage feeling overwhelmed?

What things am I avoiding because I feel overwhelmed by them?

What is one bold action I can take to begin clearing the path for action?

How does my feeling of being overwhelmed affect my self-worth?

How can I love myself more deeply in spite of feeling overwhelmed?

AFFIRMATION:

I am like the eagle soaring above the land. I see the entirety of what needs to happen to facilitate the evolution of the world. I use my perspective to see my unique and irreplaceable role in the Cosmic Plan. I see relationships and patterns that others do not always see. My perspective helps us all to build a peaceful world more effectively and in a consciously directed way.

EFT SETUP:

Even though it makes me nervous to stop "doing" and sit with the stillness, I now trust the process and know that my state of alignment and clarity with my intentions is the most powerful thing I can do to create effectively and powerfully in my life. I relax, I trust and let my abundance unfold, and I deeply and completely love and accept myself.

JUNE 29, 2022 – NEW MOON

 Cancer 7 degrees, 22 minutes

Gate 52 – The Gate of Perspective

New Moon energy invites us to explore how we can deepen our alignment with our intentions and asks us to focus on what we want to grow and expand on in our lives.

Sometimes we get so focused on a small detail, thought, or memory that we lose perspective on the bigger picture of where we need to be focusing and pointing our attention. It is easy sometimes to forget that a forest is comprised of many trees. When we simply focus on one lone tree, we are missing the main point of the forest.

This New Moon demands of us to stop and explore whether we are focusing in a direction that is supporting our growth and to ask ourselves if we need to refocus our intentions and set a new course to create what we want in our lives. Is there anything in your life that is distracting you from focusing on what you need or want to be focusing on and how can you remove whatever might be distracting you from seeing the bigger picture of where you are headed.

 CHALLENGE:

To learn to take a step back with your perspective while staying focused on the long-term goal. To listen attentively to your own inner wisdom and to follow your Human Design Strategy and Authority to determine where to put your focus.

OPTIMAL EXPRESSION:

The ability to see the bigger perspective and purpose of what is going on around you and to know exactly where to focus your energy and attention to facilitate the unfolding of what is next.

UNBALANCED EXPRESSION:

To let your ability to see the big picture cause you to get distracted by the proverbial rabbit hole. To get so deep into the details of an inconsequential factor that you lose momentum.

CONTEMPLATIONS:

What do you do to maintain and sustain your focus? Is there anything in your environment or your life that you need to move out of the way in order for you to deepen your focus?

How do you manage overwhelm? What things are you avoiding because you feel overwhelmed by them? What is one bold action you can take toward clearing the path for action?

How does your overwhelm affect your self-worth? How can you love yourself more deeply in spite of the overwhelm?

AFFIRMATION:

The stillness of my concentration allows patterns and order to be revealed to me. My understanding of this order gives me the power to continue to create effectively. The stillness of my concentration is the source of my power this week.

JULY 1, 2022

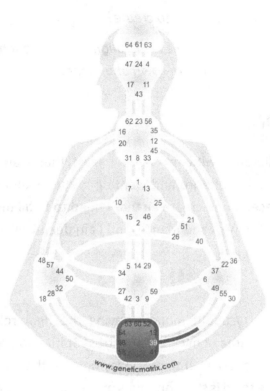

www.geneticmatrix.com

GATE 39: RECALIBRATION

CHALLENGE:

To challenge and tease out energies that are not in alignment with faith and abundance. To bring them to awareness and to use them as pushing off points to deepen faith and trust in Source.

JOURNAL QUESTIONS:

Do I trust Source?

What do I need to do to deepen my trust in Source?

Do I feel like I am enough?

Do I feel like I have enough?

Take stock of everything I have and everything I've been given. Do I have enough? Have I ever not been supported?

What do I have that I'm grateful for?

Have I abdicated my own power to create?

What needs to be healed, released, aligned, or brought to my awareness to reactivate my power to create my own abundance?

AFFIRMATION:

I am deeply calibrated with my faith. I trust that I am fully supported. I use experiences that create desire and wanting in me as opportunities to deepen my faith that I will receive and create all that I need to fulfill my mind, body, and spirit. I am in the perfect flow of abundance, and I am deeply aligned with Source.

EFT SETUP:

Even though I worry about money, having the right relationship, and creating abundance in every area of my life, I now trust Spirit and allow the abundant nature of the Universe to reveal itself to me. I stay open to the possibilities of miracles and trust that all I have to do is stay conscious of the abundance of Spirit unfolding within me, and I deeply and completely love and accept myself.

JULY 7, 2022

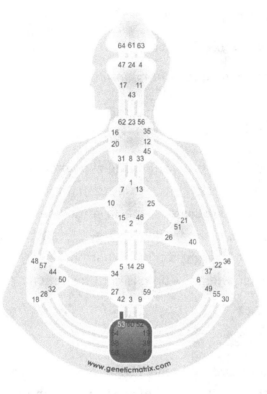

www.geneticmatrix.com

GATE 53: STARTING

CHALLENGE:

To respond in alignment with your energy blueprint to opportunities to get things started. To initiate the process of preparing or "setting the state" for the manifestation of a dream before it becomes a reality. To learn to trust in the timing of the Universe and not take charge and try to implement your own ideas while working against Divine Timing. To not burn out trying to complete things. To find peace as a "starter," not a "finisher."

JOURNAL QUESTIONS:

How do I feel about myself when I have an idea and I can't get it initiated?

How do I feel when someone takes my initial idea and builds on it?

Do I value what I started?

What identities and attachments do I have to being the one who starts and finishes something?

Do I judge myself for not finishing something?

How can I be gentler with myself?

Do I trust Divine Timing?

How can I deepen my trust in right timing?

AFFIRMATION:

I am a servant to Divine Inspiration. My thoughts, inspirations, and ideas set the stage for creative expansion and the potential for evolution. I take action on the ideas that present themselves to me in an aligned way. I honor all other ideas knowing that my gift is in the spark of energy that gets things rolling when the timing is right. While I wait for right timing, I guard my energy and charge my battery so that I am sustainable when the time is right for action.

EFT SETUP:

Even though I am scared to believe that my big dreams could come true, I now choose to trust the infinite power of the Universe and know that I am never given a dream that can't be fulfilled, and I deeply and completely love and accept myself.

JULY 13, 2022

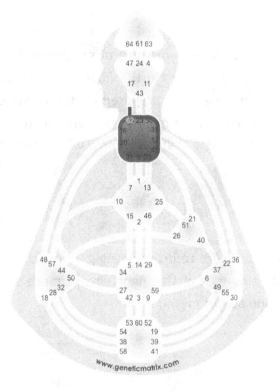

GATE 62: PREPARATION

CHALLENGE:

To trust that you will be prepared for the next step. To not let worry and over-preparation distract you from being present in the moment. To let the fear of not being ready keep you trapped.

JOURNAL QUESTIONS:

Do I worry?

What do I do to manage my worry?

What can I do to trust that I know what I need to know?

What proof do I have that I am in the flow of preparation?

Is there anything in my life right now that I need to plan for?

Am I over-planning?

Does my need for contingency plans keep me stuck?

AFFIRMATION:

I create the foundation for the practice of excellence by engineering the plan of action that creates growth. I am in the flow of my understanding, and I use my knowledge and experience to be prepared for the evolution of what is next. I am ready and I am prepared. I trust my own preparation and allow myself to be in the flow of what is next knowing that I will know what I need to know when I need to know it.

EFT SETUP:

Even though I feel pressure to do something, I now choose to relax and trust the power of my dreams to call the right circumstance to me, and I deeply and completely love and accept myself.

JULY 13, 2022 – SUPER FULL MOON

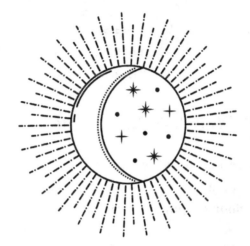

 Capricorn 21 degrees, 20 minutes

Gate 61 – The Gate of Wonder

Full moon energy invites us to explore what we need to release and let go of in order to stay in alignment with our intentions.

This Full Moon invites us to engage in our life with curiosity and wonder, to find the bigger answers to our questions and to explore tangible and practical ways to release our need to know it all, and to trust that there is a greater mystery unfolding in our lives.

We are filled with the energy of momentum and creativity. We are wanting to explore what to start but if we get too bogged down in the details or in worry, we run the risk of turning off the innocence and wonder that can keep us open to new potentials.

The Full Moon invites to you engage in your dreams with curiosity and to not let yourself stop short if you haven't worked through all the details yet. You will know what you need to know when you need to know it.

 CHALLENGE:

To learn to embrace the idea that everything happens for a reason and that even painful events can be catalytic if you allow yourself to find the blessings in the pain.

OPTIMAL EXPRESSION:

The ability to see purpose in a bigger perspective that transcends the smaller details of an experience or event. The ability to stay in a state of innocence and delusional confidence as a way of sustaining powerful creativity.

UNBALANCED EXPRESSION:

To get lost in the question "why" without allowing yourself to mine the experience for the blessings from the pain. To get so lost in an expansive perspective that you can't ground yourself in finding a practical way forward.

CONTEMPLATIONS:

What do you do to maintain your sense of wonder? How can you deepen your awe of the magnificence of the Universe?

What old thoughts, patterns, and beliefs do you need to release in order to align with your knowingness and to trust your "delusional confidence" as a powerful creative state?

AFFIRMATION:

In the stillness I surrender to the Great Mystery of Life and the Divine. I allow Divine Inspiration to wash over me, and I listen with great attention and appreciation. I trust that I receive the perfect inspiration and I simply let the inspiration flow to me. I am grateful.

JULY 19, 2022

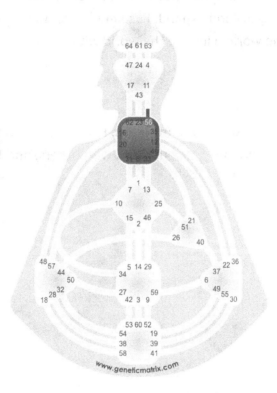

www.geneticmatrix.com

GATE 56: EXPANSION

CHALLENGE:

To learn to share stories and inspirations with the right people at the right time. To learn to tell stories of expansion and not depletion and contraction.

JOURNAL QUESTIONS:

What stories do I share repeatedly with others?

Do they lift people up or cause them to contract?

What stories do I tell about myself and my voice that cause me to either expand or contract?

What am I here to inspire others to do or be?

AFFIRMATION:

I am a Divine Storyteller. The stories of possibility that I share have the power to inspire others to grow and expand. I use my words as a template for possibility and expansion for the world. I inspire the world with my words.

EFT SETUP:

Even though I'm afraid to share my ideas, I now choose to take leadership with my inspirations and share my precious ideas with others, and I deeply and completely love and accept myself.

JULY 25, 2022

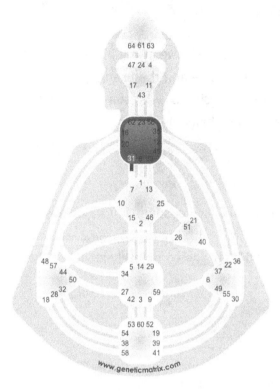

www.geneticmatrix.com

GATE 31: THE LEADER

CHALLENGE:

To learn to lead as a representative of the people you are leading. To cultivate a leadership agenda of service. To not let your fear of not being seen, heard, or accepted get in the way of healthy leadership. To learn to take your rightful place as a leader and not hide out.

JOURNAL QUESTIONS:

How do I feel about being a leader?

Am I comfortable leading?

Do I shrink from taking leadership?

What is my place of service?

Who do I serve?

AFFIRMATION:

I am a natural born leader. I serve at my highest potential when I am empowering others by giving them a voice and then serving their needs. I use my power to lead people to a greater expansion of who they are and to support them in increasing their abundance, sustainability, and peace.

EFT SETUP:

Even though I'm afraid to be seen, I now choose to express myself and the magnificence that is me with gusto, courage, awareness of my own power and preciousness, and I deeply and completely love and accept myself.

JULY 28, 2022 – NEW MOON

 Leo 5 degrees, 38 minutes

Gate 31 – The Gate of the Leader

New Moon energy invites us to explore how we can deepen our alignment with our intentions and asks us to focus on what we want to grow and expand on in our lives.

This new moon invites us to explore where we may be blocking or resisting our role as leaders and where we might be holding ourselves back from taking a leadership role in our lives.

The theme of innovation and transformation are playing out during this cycle. We are learning to trust our own knowingness and to lead with our wisdom, even if we don't have the proof that what we know is right. We are learning to trust ourselves, our insights, and our connection to our personal truth and to lead from that place of authentic alignment. What do you need to release in order to assume your natural leadership role?

 CHALLENGE:

To learn to lead as a representative for the greater good. To lead from Heart not ego.

OPTIMAL EXPRESSION:

The ability to be able to listen, learn, hear, and serve the people you lead and to assume and value your right leadership position as the voice for the people you are leading.

UNBALANCED EXPRESSION:

To take or seize leadership for personal gain. To fail to lead when it is necessary because of fear or vulnerability.

CONTEMPLATIONS:

How do I feel about my leadership ability?

When do I step joyfully into being a leader?

AFFIRMATION:

I assume my position of natural leadership when I am asked or invited to assume influence. My words, my thoughts, my ideas, and my dream are important and worthy of sharing with the right people.

JULY 31, 2022

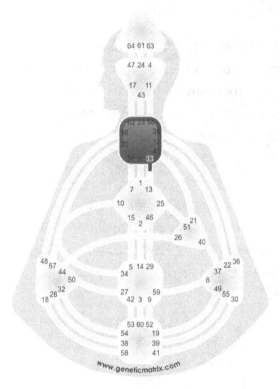

www.geneticmatrix.com

GATE 33: RETELLING

CHALLENGE:

To learn to share a personal narrative that reflects your true value and your worth. To share a personal narrative when it serves the intention to serve, improving the direction of others. To share history in an empowering way.

JOURNAL QUESTIONS:

What personal narratives am I telling that might be keeping me stuck, feeling like a victim, or feeling unlovable?

How can I rewrite these stories?

What listening practices do I have?

What can I do to listen better so that I can gauge when it is the right time to share in a powerful way?

AFFIRMATION:

I am a processor of stories. My gift is my ability to help others find the blessings, the love, and the power from stories of pain. I hold people's secrets and stories and transform them to share when the time is right. The stories I tell change the direction of people's lives. I use the power of stories to increase the power of Heart in the world and to help build a world of Love.

EFT SETUP:

Even though my stories from my past have held me back, I now choose to rewrite the story of my life and tell it the way I choose, with forgiveness, embracing the gifts, and honoring my courage and strength in my story, and I deeply and completely love and accept myself.

AUGUST 6, 2022

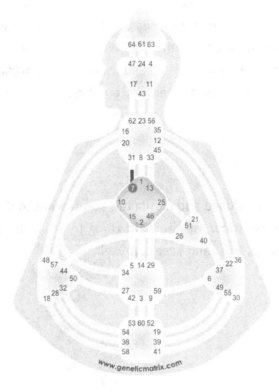

www.geneticmatrix.com

GATE 7: COLLABORATION

CHALLENGE:

To understand the need to be in front and allow yourself to serve through building teams, collaborating, and influencing the figurehead of leadership. To be at peace with serving the leader through support and collaboration. To recognize that the voice of the leader is only as strong and powerful as the support he/she receives.

JOURNAL QUESTIONS:

What are my gifts and strengths? How do I use those gifts to influence and lead others?

How do I feel about not being the figurehead of leadership?

What happens when I only support the leadership? Do I still feel powerful? Influential?

Make a list of the times when my influence has positively directed leadership.

AFFIRMATION:

I am an agent of peace who influences the direction and organization of leadership. I unify people around ideas. I influence with my wisdom, my knowledge, and my connections. I am a team builder, a collaborator, and I organize people in ways that empower them and support them in creating a collective direction rooted in compassion.

EFT SETUP:

Even though I feel confused and conflicted about what to do, I trust the Divine Flow and let the Universe show me the right thing to do in the right time, and I deeply and completely love, trust and accept myself.

AUGUST 12, 2022

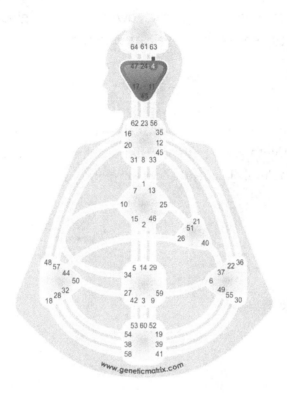

GATE 4: POSSIBILITY

CHALLENGE:

To learn to embrace ideas as possibilities, not answers, and to let the power of the possibility stimulate the imagination as a way of calibrating the emotions and the Heart. This Gate teaches us the power of learning to wait to see which possibility actually manifests in the physical world and to experiment with options in response.

JOURNAL QUESTIONS:

What ideas do I have right now that need me to nurture and activate them?

What possibilities do these ideas stimulate right now? Take some time to write or visualize the possibilities.

Am I comfortable with waiting? What can I do to increase my patience and curiosity?

AFFIRMATION:

I am tuned into the cosmic flow of possibility. I am inspired about exploring new possibilities and potentials. I use the power of my thoughts to stretch the limits of what is known and engage my imagination to explore the potential of the unknown.

EFT SETUP:

Even though I don't know what to do, I allow my questions to seed the Universe and I trust and wait with great patience that the answers will be revealed to me, and I deeply and completely love and accept myself.

AUGUST 12, 2022 – FULL MOON

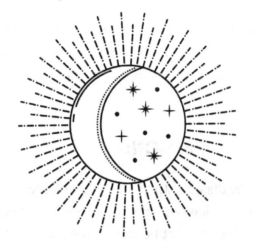

 Aquarius 19 degrees, 21 minutes

Gate 49 – The Gate of the Catalyst

Full moon energy invites us to explore what we need to release and let go of in order to stay in alignment with our intentions.

We've been seeking answers. The pressure to figure out the solutions to our challenges can make us vulnerable to using our minds instead of trusting our wisdom and our connection to Life's Intelligence for the understanding that we seek.

This Full Moon invites us to release anything that is keeping us from seeing the Truth, especially in our relationships. Be prepared this week to become more clear, more aligned, and to have a greater understanding of what changes you need to make to proclaim and defend your value.

With this energy, we are releasing old relationship patterns and rewriting our relationship agreements. We are releasing old agreements that have caused us to settle for less than our true value and for circumstances that do no reflects our values. Be prepared for big changes.

 ## CHALLENGE:

To not let your sensitivity to others cause you to give up your own needs and wants or to retreat from the world. To be compassionate but not co-dependent. To learn how to craft true intimacy and emotional connection.

OPTIMAL EXPRESSION:

The ability to sense the emotional needs of others and your community and know how to bring the emotional energy back into alignment with sufficiency and sustainability. The ability to be emotionally vulnerable and present to increase Heart to Heart connections.

UNBALANCED EXPRESSION:

To be so emotionally dialed in to others that you give up what you want or fail to ask for what you need. To hide out from the overwhelm because you're too sensitive. To fail to deal with truth or conflict because it feels too emotionally challenging.

CONTEMPLATIONS:

What cycles in my life are coming to an end? Am I resisting or allowing these conclusions? Is there anything I need to do to create space for the beginning of a new cycle?

What lessons have I learned from this cycle? Which blessings am I taking with me into the new cycle? Where do I have new clarity?

What does intimacy mean to me? Are my needs being met? Am I meeting the needs of my partner? Am I asking clearly for what I want? Am I allowing my partner to give to me? Are there places where I need to understand fulfilling my own intimacy needs?

AFFIRMATION:

I am deeply aware of the emotional needs and energy of others. My sensitivity and awareness give me insights that allow me to create intimacy and vulnerability in my relationships. I am aware and attuned to the emotional frequency around me, and I make adjustments to help support a high frequency of emotional alignment. I honor my own emotional needs as the foundation of what I share with others.

AUGUST 17, 2022

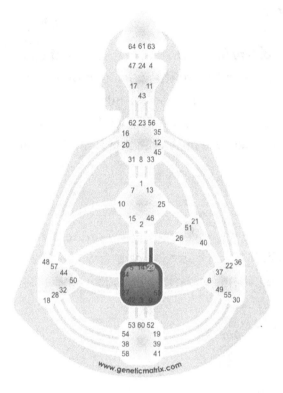

www.geneticmatrix.com

GATE 29: DEVOTION

CHALLENGE:

To discover what and who you need to devote yourself to. To sustain yourself so that you can sustain your devotion. To learn to say no to what you need to say no to and to learn to yes to what you want to say yes to.

JOURNAL QUESTIONS:

What devotion do I have right now that drives me?

Is this a devotion that inspires me, or do I feel overly obligated to it?

Who would I be and what would I choose if I gave myself permission to say no more often?

What would I like to say no to that I am saying yes to right now?

What obligations do I need to take off my plate right now?

What would I like to devote myself to?

AFFIRMATION:

I have an extraordinary ability to devote myself to the manifestation of an idea. My commitment to my story and to the fulfillment of my intention changes the story of what is possible in my own life and for humanity. I choose my commitments with great care. I devote myself to what is vital for the evolution of the world, and I nurture myself first because my well-being is the foundation of what I create.

EFT SETUP:

Even though I am afraid to invest all my effort into my dream... what if it fails... what if I'm crazy... what if I just need to buckle down and be "normal"... I now choose to do it anyway, and I deeply and completely love and accept myself.

AUGUST 23, 2022

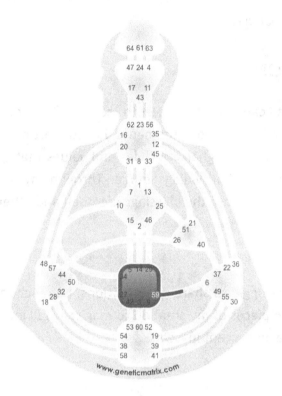

www.geneticmatrix.com

GATE 59: SUSTAINABILITY

CHALLENGE:

To learn to make abundant choices that sustain you, and at the same time, others. To collaborate and initiate others into sustainable relationships from a place of sufficiency. To learn to share what you have in a sustainable way.

JOURNAL QUESTIONS:

Do I trust in my own abundance?

How do I feel about sharing what I have with others?

Am I creating relationship and partnership agreements that honor my work?

Do I have relationships and agreements that are draining me? What needs to change?

How do I feel about being "right"?

Am I open to other ways of thinking or being?

Do I believe in creating agreements and alignments with people who have different values and perspectives?

AFFIRMATION:

The energy that I carry has the power to create sufficiency and sustainability for all. I craft valuable alliances and agreements that support me in expanding abundance for everyone. I hold to higher principles and values that are rooted in my trust in sufficiency and the all-providing Source. Through my work and alignments my blessings serve to increase the blessings of myself and others.

EFT SETUP:

Even though I struggle to share my intentions, I now choose to boldly state them and wait for the pieces of my creation to magically fall into place, and I deeply and completely love and accept myself.

AUGUST 27, 2022 – NEW MOON

Virgo 4 degrees, 3 minutes

Gate 59 – The Gate of Sustainability

New Moon energy invites us to explore how we can deepen our alignment with our intentions and asks us to focus on what we want to grow and expand on in our lives.

The hope of the New Moon cycle invites us into the possibility of refraining our definition of abundance and sufficiency. We are learning to trust that there is always enough.

We are setting intention in this cycle to increase our ability to create more and to create sustainably so that we can better fulfill our purpose, serve at our highest level, and also be able to provide for our loved ones.

This New Moon invites us to open new portals of faith and to do the right thing. We're deepening our connection to Source and learning to find the balance between BE-ing and DO-ing.

CHALLENGE:

To learn to trust that there is enough. To share what you have without depleting yourself. To be employed creating sustainable resources for others. To do work that helps you take care of the people you love.

OPTIMAL EXPRESSION:

To trust in sufficiency and to know that when you create abundance there is great fulfillment in sharing. To craft partnerships and relationships that sustain you and the foundation of your lives.

UNBALANCED EXPRESSION:

To manipulate, steal or overcompensate for a perceived lack of resources. To fight, hoard, and try to take more than your fair share because you fail to believe in sufficiency. To defend the belief that there is not enough.

CONTEMPLATIONS:

Meditate (and journal) this week on what avenues of impact would best serve you, your intentions, and your business. What is the next step in creating your intentions and your dreams? Where do you need to "get to work" to be ready for things to manifest?

AFFIRMATION:

I radiate my desires into the Universe and impregnate the ethers with my dreams. My intentions influence the right people, the right places, the right circumstances, and the right opportunities at the perfect time, and I know that I am radiating pure joyful intention all the time.

AUGUST 29, 2022

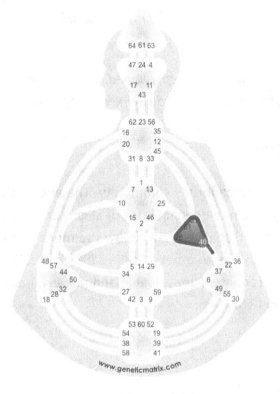

GATE 40: RESTORATION

CHALLENGE:

To learn to value yourself enough to retreat from community and the energy of those you love to restore, restock, and replenish your inner resources. To learn to interpret the signal of loneliness correctly. To take responsibility for your own care and resources and to not abdicate your own power to take care of yourself.

JOURNAL QUESTIONS:

What role does loneliness play in my life?

Has loneliness caused me to doubt my value?

What do I need to do to restore my energy?

Am I doing enough to take care of myself?

What agreements am I making in my relationships that might be causing me to compromise my value?

How can I rewrite these agreements?

Am I abdicating my responsibility for my self-care?

Am I living a "martyr" model?

What needs to be healed, released, aligned, and brought to my awareness for me to take responsibility for cultivating my own sense of value and my self-worth?

AFFIRMATION:

I am a powerful resource for my community. The energy that I hold impacts others deeply and brings them to deeper states of alignment and sustainability. I take care of my body, mind, and soul because I know the more that I am and the more that I have, the more I can give to others. I take care of myself first because I know that good things flow from me. I am valuable and powerful, and I claim and defend the true story of Who I Truly Am.

EFT SETUP:

Even though it is hard to let go of the obligations of relationships, I now choose to release all relationships that are draining and unsupportive, and I deeply and completely love and accept myself.

SEPTEMBER 4, 2022

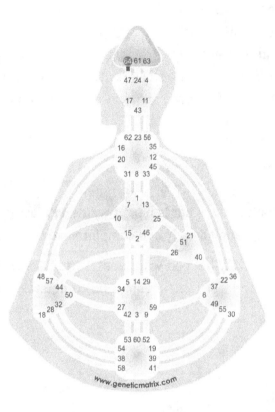

www.geneticmatrix.com

GATE 64: DIVINE TRANSFERENCE

CHALLENGE:

To not let the power of your big ideas overwhelm you and shut down your dreaming and creating. To not get lost in the pressure of answering the how question .

JOURNAL QUESTIONS:

What do I do to take care of my Big Ideas?

How do I feel about having dreams but not always the solutions?

How can I stop judging the gift of my dreams?

Do I trust that the how of my ideas will be revealed? How can I deepen this trust?

AFFIRMATION:

I am a conduit for expansive thinking. My inspirations and ideas create the seeds of possibility in my mind and in the mind of others. I honor the dreams that pass through my mind and allow my big ideas to stimulate my imagination and the imagination of others. I trust the Universe to reveal the details of my dreams when the time is right. I use the power of my dreams to stimulate a world of possibility and expansion.

EFT SETUP:

Even though I don't know what is next, I wait and trust that the perfect right step will show up for me, and I deeply and completely love and accept myself.

Even though I feel overwhelmed with ideas, I trust the Universe to reveal the next step to me. I relax and wait, and I deeply and completely love and accept myself.

SEPTEMBER 10, 2022

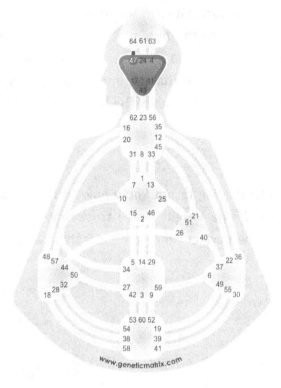

www.geneticmatrix.com

GATE 47: MINDSET

CHALLENGE:

To become skilled at a mindset of open-ness and possibility. To not let inspiration die because you don't know how to fulfill it.

JOURNAL QUESTIONS:

What thoughts do I have when I receive an idea or inspiration?

Am I hopeful or despairing?

How does it feel to let go of figuring out how I'm going to make my idea a reality?

What do I do to regulate my mindset?

What practices do I need to cultivate to increase the power of my thoughts?

AFFIRMATION:

My mindset is the source of my inspired actions and attitude. I know that when I receive an idea and inspiration it is my job to nurture the idea by using the power of my imagination to increase the potential and emotional frequency of the idea. I consistently keep my inner and outer environment aligned with the energy of possibility and potential. I know that it is my job to create by virtue of my alignment, and I relax knowing that it is the job of the Universe to fulfill my inspirations.

EFT SETUP:

Even though it is frustrating to not know how to make something happen, I now choose to wait for Divine Insight, and I trust that the right information will be revealed to me at the perfect time, and I deeply and completely love and accept myself.

SEPTEMBER 10, 2022 – FULL MOON

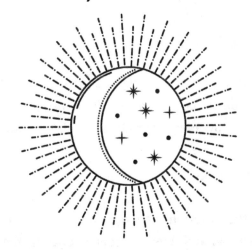

 Pisces 17 degrees, 40 minutes
Gate 22 – The Gate of Surrender

Full moon energy invites us to explore what we need to release and let go of in order to stay in alignment with our intentions.

This Full Moon invites to explore our mindset and to assess whether our thinking is supporting us in relaxing and trusting that the process of whatever we are creating is unfolding perfectly. Our mindset is juxtaposed with the theme of surrender. When we have positive expectations and we have released ourselves from the pressure of figuring things out, then we can relax and let the story unfold.

Obviously, if we are struggling with our mindset, we may feel that we need to power through the reality of the situation and use our sheer force and will to try to make things turn out the way we hope.

 CHALLENGE:

To have the courage to follow your passion and know that you will be supported. To learn to surrender and trust in your support.

 OPTIMAL EXPRESSION:

The grace to know that you are fully supported by the Universal flow of abundance and to pursue your passion and your unique contribution to the world no matter what. To trust that you will be given what you need when you need it in order to make your unique contribution to the world.

UNBALANCED EXPRESSION:

To hold yourself back from following your truth and your passion because you are afraid that it won't be supported, or it will be meaningless. To use drama as a way of distracting yourself or avoiding your alignment with your creative passion.

CONTEMPLATIONS:

When faced with the emotional energy and drama of others what is my strategy to allow and be aware? What are my strategies for detaching?

Do I trust that my passions and the fulfillment of my creative desires are supported? What old ideas do I need to surrender to allow myself to follow my passion, and trust the direction that they will lead me?

AFFIRMATION:

In the face of Divine Order, I stand with Grace and presence. I see, integrate, evaluate, and share my awareness. I articulate the conclusions with Grace and correct timing. I use my ability to perceive correct awareness to bring my awareness and understandings to others. I am the calm within the storm. I follow my passion with the awareness that I am fully supported and that my alignment with my creative expression is the gift I am here to share with the world.

SEPTEMBER 15, 2022

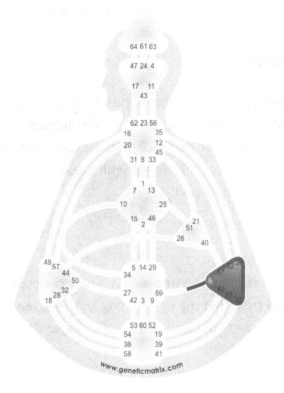

www.geneticmatrix.com

GATE 6: IMPACT

CHALLENGE:

To become proficient in using emotional energy and learn to trust that your impact is in service to the world. When you understand that your life is a vehicle for service and your energy is being used to influence and impact those around you, you assume greater obligation and responsibility to maintaining a high frequency of energy. The quality of the emotional energy you cultivate influences others to come together in an equitable, sustainable, and peaceful way. Learning to trust that your words and impact will have effect when the timing is correct and not overriding Divine Timing.

JOURNAL QUESTIONS:

What do I need to do to deepen my trust in Divine Timing?

What do I need to do to prepare myself to be seen and to have influence?

What do I need to do to sustain my emotional energy in order to align with peaceful and sustainable solutions?

How do I feel about lack? How do I feel about abundance? How can I create a greater degree of emotional abundance in my life? In my daily practice?

AFFIRMATION:

My emotional energy influences the world around me. I am rooted in the energy of equity, sustainability, and peace. When I am aligned with abundance, I am an energetic source of influence that facilitates elegant solutions to creating peace and well-being. I am deliberate and aligned with values that create peace in my life, in my community, and in the world.

EFT SETUP:

Even though I am ready to leap into action, I now choose to take a breath, wait out my emotions, and trust that the right timing will be revealed to me. I'm not missing out on anything. Divine Order is the rule of the day, and I deeply and completely love and accept myself.

SEPTEMBER 21, 2022

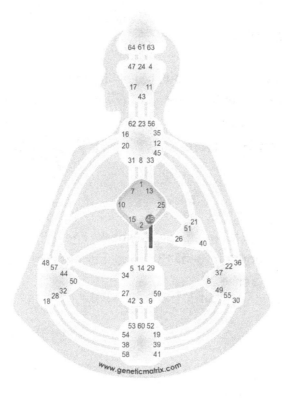

www.geneticmatrix.com

GATE 46: EMBODIMENT

CHALLENGE:

To learn to love your body. To learn to fully be in your body. To learn to love the sensual nature of your physical form and to move it with love and awareness.

JOURNAL QUESTIONS:

Do I love my body?

What can I do to deepen my love for my body?

What parts of my body do I love and appreciate?

Make a list of every part of my body that I love.

What do I need to do to amplify the life force I am experiencing in my body?

What kinds of devotion and commitment do I experience that help me harness greater amounts of life force in my body?

How can I deepen my commitment and devotion to my body?

 ## AFFIRMATION:

My body is the vehicle for my soul. My ability to fully express who I am (and my life and soul purpose) is deeply rooted in my body's ability to carry my soul. I love, nurture, and commit to my body. I appreciate all of its miraculous abilities and form. Every day I love my body more.

 ## EFT SETUP:

Even though it is hard for me to love my body, I now choose to embrace my amazing physical form and honor it for all the good it brings me, and I deeply and completely love and accept myself.

SEPTEMBER 25, 2022 – NEW MOON

 Libra 2 degrees, 48 minutes
Gate 46 – The Gate of Embodiment

New Moon energy invites us to explore how we can deepen our alignment with our intentions and asks us to focus on what we want to grow and expand on in our lives.

This New Moon invites us to begin a new healthy relationship with our bodies. The Gate 46 reminds that our body is a vehicle for our Soul. Without a healthy vehicle, it is hard to fulfill our Soul Purpose.

The New Moon is also about invoking a state of presence into your life. What do you need to do to be more present, be more in your body? Are there distractions and habits that you've cultivated that might be keeping you from being fully present to all that your life is offering you?

 ## CHALLENGE:

To learn to love and take care of your body. To learn to deeply appreciate the body as a servant to the soul.

 ## OPTIMAL EXPRESSION:

To recognize that the body is the vehicle for the soul and to love the body as a vital element of the soul's expression in life. To nurture, be grounded in, and fully care for the body. To savor the physicality of the human experience. To explore how to fully embody the spirit in your body and to be committed and devoted to seeing how much life force you can embody into your physical form.

UNBALANCED EXPRESSION:

To hate your body. To fail to be "in" your body. To neglect or fail to take care of your body. To ignore the messages your body is giving you.

CONTEMPLATIONS:

What is my reality telling me? Are there messages I need to heed?

What discourages me? Do I push or do I allow? What do I need to do to allow rather than think my way through something?

What do I need to do to take better care of my body? How can I love my body more?

AFFIRMATION:

Physical reality is an expression of my consciousness. I look to my reality to mirror my mindset and my beliefs back to me. I am clear, conscious, and awake. I am aware that I can adjust my mindset to create any physical experience I choose. I take guided actions that are in alignment with my beliefs, and I celebrate this gift of being alive in a physical body!

SEPTEMBER 27, 2022

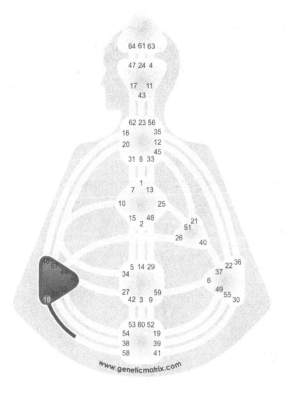

www.geneticmatrix.com

GATE 18: RE-ALIGNMENT

CHALLENGE:

To learn to wait for the right timing and the right circumstances to offer your intuitive insights into how to fix or correct a pattern. To wait for the right time and the right reason to share your critique. To understand that the purpose of re-alignment is to create more joy, not to be "right."

JOURNAL QUESTIONS:

What does joy mean to me? How do I serve it?

How do I cultivate joy in my own life?

How does it feel to be "right" about something and keep it to myself?

Do I need to release any old stories about needing to be right?

Do I trust my own insights? Do I have the courage to share them when it is necessary?

AFFIRMATION:

I am a powerful force that re-aligns patterns. My insights and awareness give people the information they need to deepen their expertise and to experience greater joy. I serve joy and I align the patterns of the world to increase the world's potential for living in the flow of joy.

EFT SETUP:

Even though I feel criticized and judged, I now choose to hear the wisdom of the correction and release my personal attachment, and I deeply and completely love and accept myself.

OCTOBER 3, 2022

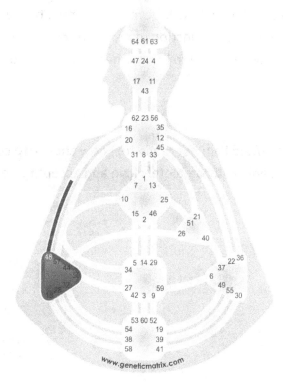

www.geneticmatrix.com

GATE 48: WISDOM

CHALLENGE:

To allow yourself to trust that you will know what you need to know when you need to know it. To not let the fear of not knowing stop you from creating. To not let not knowing hold you back.

JOURNAL QUESTIONS:

Do I trust my own knowing?

What needs to be healed, released, aligned, and brought to my awareness for me to deepen my self-trust?

What practice do I have that keeps me connected to the wisdom of Source?

How can I deepen my connection to Source?

AFFIRMATION:

I am a depth of wisdom and knowledge. My studies and experiences have taught me everything I need to know. I push beyond the limits of my earthly knowledge and take great leaps of faith as a function of my deep connection to Source knowing that I will always know what I need to know when I need to know it.

EFT SETUP:

Even though I am afraid I am not ready to, I now choose to courageously dive in and just do it, and I deeply and completely love and accept myself.

OCTOBER 8, 2022

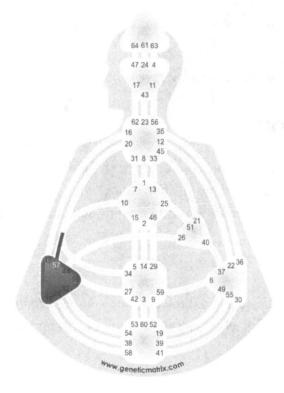

GATE 57: INSTINCT

CHALLENGE:

To learn to trust your own insights and gut. To learn to tell the difference between an instinctive response versus a fear of the future. To become skilled at your connection to your sense of right timing.

JOURNAL QUESTIONS:

Do I trust my intuition?

What does my intuition feel like to me?

Sometimes doing a retrospective analysis of my intuition/instinct makes it more clear how my intuitive signal works. What experiences in the past have I had that I knew I should or shouldn't do?

How have I experienced my intuition in the past?

When I think about moving forward in my life, do I feel afraid?

What am I afraid of? What can I do to mitigate the fear?

What impulses am I experiencing that are telling me to prepare for what is next in my life?

Am I acting on my impulses? Why or why not?

AFFIRMATION:

My Inner Wisdom is deeply connected to the pulse of Divine Timing. I listen to my Inner Wisdom and follow my instinct. I know when and how to prepare the way for the future. I take guided action and I trust myself and Source.

EFT SETUP:

Even though it is scary to trust my gut, I now choose to honor my awareness, quiet my mind, and go with what feels right, and I deeply and completely love and accept myself.

OCTOBER 9, 2022 – FULL MOON

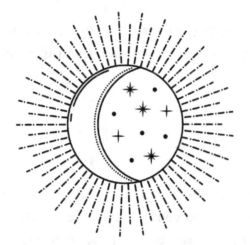

 Aries 16 degrees, 32 minutes

Gate 51– The Gate of Initiation

Full moon energy invites us to explore what we need to release and let go of in order to stay in alignment with our intentions.

The energy of this Full Moon may feel a little challenging for some of us. We are being invited to release ourselves from our old identities, the shadow of our Ego, and all those old ways we thought we needed to prove our value in the world.

This Full Moon is bringing us a death of sorts. We are dying to our old identity and emerging, in the light of the Moon, into an expanded identity that is more in alignment with our Authentic Self and our Higher Purpose.

Be prepared for things to be a little unexpected. The Moon is conspiring to shine her light on all the ways that you hold yourself back from fulfilling your True Purpose. The purpose of this revelation is to usher in a new way of living that is more in sync with your role as a leader and a healer. You're being invited to let go of all of your old identities that are keeping you playing small and holding you back from your Higher Purpose.

 CHALLENGE:

To learn to be resilient and pivot in the face of the unexpected. To not let the unexpected cause you to lose faith. To use your personal challenges to help to awaken others to faith and possibility.

OPTIMAL EXPRESSION:

The ability to consciously use cycles of disruption and unexpected twists and turns of faith as catalysts that deepen your connection to Source and to your Life and Soul Purpose.

UNBALANCED EXPRESSION:

To use shock or to be shocking as a way of getting attention. To let the unexpected cause you to lose faith and your direction. To get stuck on trying to go back to how things were before an unexpected shift and change.

CONTEMPLATIONS:

What are the lessons that I have learned from shock? How have I transformed shock into strength? How has shock initiated me into the Love of Spirit?

Where have I been shocked in ways that I need to transmute into the Love of Spirit? What trauma and drama from the shock do I need to release? How has the shock revealed to me a deeper truth and brought me to a greater awareness of Spirit? What do I need to do to move into gratitude?

AFFIRMATION:

I have the inner strength to deflect all outer shock. I am the manifestation of Spirit in form. I am a courageous, steadfast, and open to the expansion of Spirit within me. My faith and courage inspire and initiate others. My vibration is high, and I lift others up with the Truth of Spirit within me.

OCTOBER 14, 2022

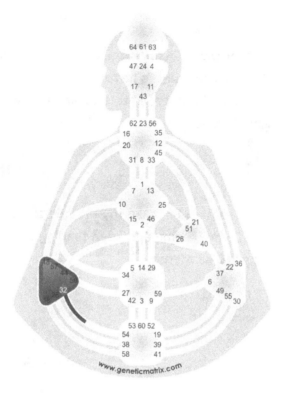

GATE 32: ENDURANCE

CHALLENGE:

To trust in Divine Timing. To prepare for the next step of manifestation and to align with the unfolding of the process. To be patient.

JOURNAL QUESTIONS:

What do I need to do to be prepared to manifest my vision?

What actionable steps need to be completed in order for me to be ready when the timing is right?

What do I need to do to cultivate patience?

Do I have a fear of failing that is causing me to avoid being prepared?

Am I over-doing and being overly prepared?

Am I pushing too hard?

What can I let go of?

AFFIRMATION:

I am a divine translator for Divine Inspiration. I sense and know what needs to be prepared on the earthly plane in order to be ready for right timing. I am aligned with right timing, and I prepare and wait patiently knowing that when the time is right, I am ready to do the work to help transform pain into power.

EFT SETUP:

Even though I have worked hard to make my dreams come true and nothing has happened yet, I trust in Divine Timing and keep tending to my vision, and I deeply and completely love and accept myself.

OCTOBER 20, 2022

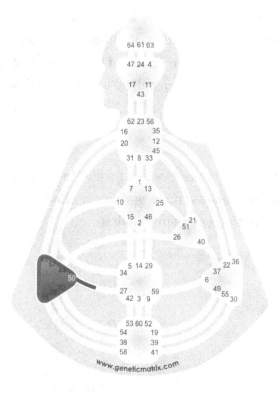

GATE 50: NURTURING

CHALLENGE:

To transcend guilt and unhealthy obligation and do what you need to do to take care of yourself in order to better serve others. To hold to rigid principles to judge others.

JOURNAL QUESTIONS:

How do I feel about taking care of myself first?

How do I sustain my nurturing energy?

What role does guilt play in driving and/or motivating me?

What would I choose if I could remove the guilt?

Do I have non-negotiable values? What are they?

How do I handle people who share different values from me?

137

AFFIRMATION:

My presence brings Love into the room. I nurture and love others. I take care of myself first in order to be better able to serve Love. I intuitively know what people need and I facilitate for them a state of self-love and self-empowerment by helping them align more deeply with the power of Love. I let go and I allow others to learn from what I model and teach. I am a deep well of love that sustains the planet.

EFT SETUP:

Even though it is hard for me to give and receive love, I now choose to be completely open to receiving and sharing deep and unconditional love starting by deeply and completely loving and accepting myself first.

OCTOBER 25, 2022

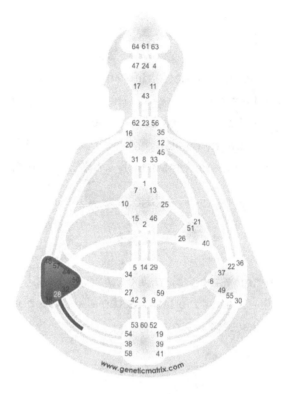

www.geneticmatrix.com

GATE 28: ADVENTURE/CHALLENGE

CHALLENGE:

To not let struggle and challenge leave you feeling defeated and despairing. To learn to face life as an adventure. Do not let challenge and struggle cause you to feel as if you have failed.

JOURNAL QUESTIONS:

How can I turn my challenge into adventure?

Where do I need to cultivate a sense of adventure in my life?

What do I need to do to rewrite the story of my "failures"?

What meanings, blessings, and lessons have I learned from my challenges?

What needs to be healed, released, aligned, and brought to my awareness for me to trust myself and my choices?

What do I need to do to forgive myself for my perceived past failures?

AFFIRMATION:

I am here to push the boundaries of life and what is possible. I thrive in situations that challenge me. I am an explorer on the leading edge of consciousness and my job is to test how far I can go. I embrace challenge. I am an adventurer. I share all that I have learned from my challenges with the world. My stories help give people greater meaning, teach them what is truly worthy of creating, and inspire people to transform.

EFT SETUP:

Even though everything feels hard, I now trust that I am learning what is truly important in my life. I trust the lessons the Universe brings me, and I deeply and completely love and accept myself.

OCTOBER 25, 2022
NEW MOON AND PARTIAL SOLAR ECLIPSE

Scorpio 2 degrees, 7 minutes – New Moon
Scorpio 1 degree, 59 minutes – Eclipse
Gate 50 – The Gate of Nurturing – New Moon
Gate 28 – The Gate of Challenge – Eclipse

New Moon energy invites us to explore how we can deepen our alignment with our intentions and asks us to focus on what we want to grow and expand on in our lives.

Eclipse energy amplifies the intensity of the New Moon.

This super intense New Moon initiates us into a powerful new cycle of growth and expansion. The Sun is pushing on us to clarify what is truly worth fighting for. This can be a somewhat challenging energy that doesn't always guarantee success on the first try. This is the energy of momentum that often time reveals the obstacles ahead, helping us gauge our direction, and our commitment to our right path.

With the New Moon highlighting the Gate 50, we are exploring our values. We are exploring our values, what we consider to be valuable, and making sure that our relationships and commitments reflect that value. This same energy invites us to explore whether we ourselves are sustainable. Taking care of ourselves is essential for us to be able to take care of others in a healthy way.

On a collective level, this energy represents rules and laws. We are assessing whether the old structures and regulations truly meet the needs of the greater good. If no, it is a vital time to begin to rewrite the old rules and implement new structures in place that are more equitable and just.

CHALLENGE:

To learn to nurture in an empowering way. To not deplete yourself in the name of nurturing others. To not let your fear of letting other people down (or suffering the consequences of their own actions) cause you to overcompensate or feel guilty.

OPTIMAL EXPRESSION:

The ability to nurture yourself so that you have more to give others. The intuition to know what others need to bring them into greater alignment with Love. To teach and share what you have to increase the wellbeing of others.

UNBALANCED EXPRESSION:

To over-nurture to the point of burnout. To care to the point of overtaking. To let guilt cause you to make commitments that do not feel good or aligned.

CONTEMPLATIONS:

What new rules do I need to play by? Do I need to create new rules in my relationships, my business, for my health, wealth, and welfare?

Do I love myself? Do I need to nurture myself more? Do I have the strength and foundation to love freely? Do I feel safe in love?

AFFIRMATION:

I establish the rules for my reality. I take care and nourish myself so that I may take care and nourish others. Everything I do for others, I do for myself first in order to sustain my energy and power. I rule with self-love and then love freely.

OCTOBER 31, 2022

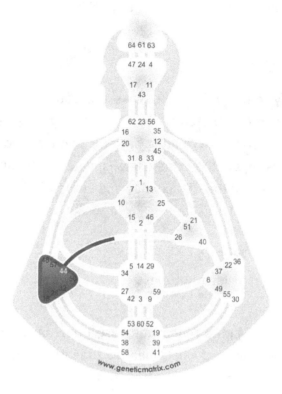

GATE 44: TRUTH

CHALLENGE:

To not get stuck in past patterns. To cultivate the courage to go forward without being stuck in the fear of the past. To learn how to transform pain into power and to have the courage to express your authentic self without compromising or settling.

JOURNAL QUESTIONS:

What patterns from the past are holding me back from moving forward with courage?

Do I see how my experiences from the past have helped me learn more about Who I Truly Am?

What have I learned about my value and my power?

What needs to be healed, released, aligned, and brought to my awareness for me to fully activate my power?

What needs to be healed, released, aligned, and brought to my awareness for me to step boldly into my aligned and authentic path?

AFFIRMATION:

I am powerfully intuitive and can sense the patterns that keep others stuck in limiting beliefs and constricted action. Through my insights and awareness, I help others break free from past limiting patterns and learn to find the power in their pain, find the blessings in their challenges, and help them align more deeply with an authentic awareness of their True Value and Purpose.

EFT SETUP:

Even though it is hard for me to let go, I deeply and completely love and accept myself.

Even though I am afraid to repeat the past, I now move forward with confidence trusting that I have learned what I needed to learn. I can create whatever future I desire, and I deeply and completely love and accept myself.

NOVEMBER 6, 2022

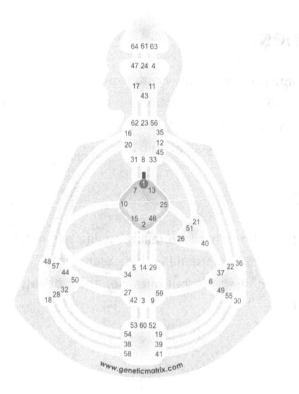

www.geneticmatrix.com

GATE 1: PURPOSE

CHALLENGE:

To discover a personal, meaningful, and world-changing narrative that aligns with a sense of purpose and mission. "I am..." To learn to love yourself enough to honor the idea that your life is the canvas, and you are the artist. What you create with your life IS the contribution you give the world.

JOURNAL QUESTIONS:

Am I fully expressing my authentic self?

What needs to be healed, released, aligned, or brought to my awareness for me to deeply express my authentic self?

Where am I already expressing who I am?

Where have I settled or compromised? What needs to change?

Do I feel connected to my life purpose? What do I need to do to deepen that connection?

AFFIRMATION:

My life is an integral part of the cosmos and the Divine Plan. I honor my life and know that the full expression of who I am is the purpose of my life. The more I am who I am, the more I create a frequency of energy that supports others in doing the same. I commit to exploring all of who I am.

EFT SETUP:

Even though I am afraid that I am failing my life mission, I now choose to relax and allow my life to unfold before me with ease and grace. I trust that every step I take is perfectly aligned with my soul purpose, and I deeply and completely love and accept myself.

NOVEMBER 8, 2022
FULL MOON AND LUNAR ECLIPSE

 Taurus 15 degrees, 59 minutes – Full Moon

Taurus 16 degrees, 00 minutes – Eclipse

Gate 2 – The Gate of Allowing

Full moon energy invites us to explore what we need to release and let go of in order to stay in alignment with our intentions. Eclipse energy amplifies the intensity of the Full Moon.

This amplified Full Moon delivers a powerful call to release anything that is blocking you from receiving all that you deserve. There is a direct relationship between your sense of value, your self-worth, and what you are willing to allow yourself to receive.

This Full Moon invited you to explore how much good are you willing to allow. How receptive are you to support and resources that continue to give you all that you need to be the full expression of all of who you are?

 ## CHALLENGE:

To learn to value yourself so that you will delegate the things that are not yours to do and allow others to help and support you. To learn to trust in the goodness of the Universe enough so that you know you are fully supported. To learn that you are worthy of support.

OPTIMAL EXPRESSION:

To value yourself enough to allow yourself to receive all the support and resources you need to fulfill your life purpose.

UNBALANCED EXPRESSION:

To push help away, to fail to delegate, or to do everything yourself because you don't believe that you are worthy of support. To fail to take the actions that you need to take to ensure your support because you don't trust in your own value enough to believe that you are worthy of success.

CONTEMPLATIONS:

How good are you at letting others help and support you?

Do you value yourself enough to allow yourself to be supported?

Do you think you deserve to be supported? What beliefs need to shift or change in order for you to believe that you are worthy of support?

AFFIRMATION:

I am an irreplaceable and vital part of the world. My life and my purpose are inherently valuable, and I bring to the world something that no one else has ever brought before and will never bring again. To fulfill the story of who I am, I trust in and allow myself to receive all the support I need to do what I came here to do.

NOVEMBER 11, 2022

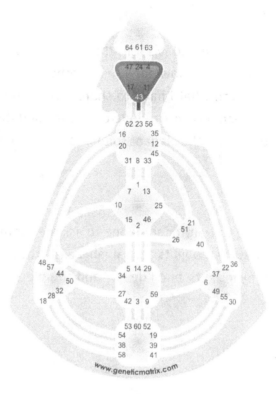

GATE 43: INSIGHT

CHALLENGE:

To be comfortable and to trust epiphanies and deep inner knowing without doubting what you know. To trust that when the timing is right you will know how to share what you know and serve your role as a transformative messenger who has insights that can change the way people think and what they know.

JOURNAL QUESTIONS:

Do I trust in Divine Timing?

Do I trust myself and my own Inner Knowing?

What can I do to deepen my connection with my Source of Knowing?

What needs to be healed, released, aligned, or brought to my awareness for me to trust my own Inner Knowing?

AFFIRMATION:

I am a vessel of knowledge and wisdom that has the ability to transform the way people think. I share my knowledge with others when they are ready and vibrationally aligned with what I have to share. When the time is right, I have the right words, and the right insights to help others expand their thinking, re-calibrate their mindset, and discover the elegant solutions to the challenges facing Humanity.

EFT SETUP:

Even though it is hard to wait for someone to ask me for my insights, I now choose to wait and know that my thoughts are valuable and precious. I only share them with people who value my insights, and I deeply and completely love and accept myself.

NOVEMBER 17, 2022

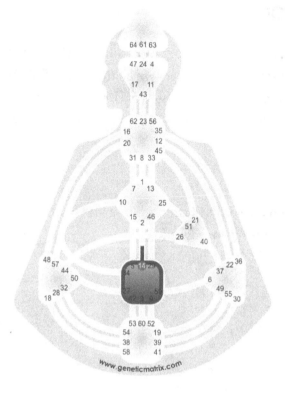

GATE 14: CREATION

CHALLENGE:

To learn to trust to respond to opportunities that bring resources instead of forcing them or overworking. To learn to value resources and to appreciate how easily they can be created when you are aligned. To be gracious and grateful and not take for granted the resources you have.

JOURNAL QUESTIONS:

Do I trust that I am supported?

Am I doing my "right" work?

What is the work that feels aligned with my purpose?

How is that work showing up in my life right now?

What resources do I have right now that I need to be grateful for?

If I didn't need the money, what work would I be doing?

AFFIRMATION:

I am in the flow of Divine Support. When I trust the generous nature of the Divine and I cultivate a state of faith, I receive all the opportunities and support that I need to evolve my life and transform the world. I know that the right work shows up for me, and I am fulfilled in the expression of my life force energy.

EFT SETUP:

Even though I am afraid that I cannot do what I love and make money, I deeply and completely love and accept myself.

NOVEMBER 22, 2022

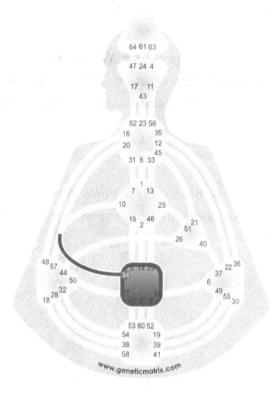

www.geneticmatrix.com

GATE 34: POWER

CHALLENGE:

To learn to measure out energy in order to stay occupied and busy but to not burn yourself out trying to force the timing or the "rightness" of a project. To wait to know which project or creation to implement based on when you get something to respond to.

JOURNAL QUESTIONS:

Do I trust in Divine Timing?

What do I need to do to deepen my trust?

How do I cultivate greater patience in my life?

What fears come up for me when I think of waiting?

How can I learn to wait with greater faith and ease?

What do I do to occupy myself while I'm waiting?

AFFIRMATION:

I am a powerful servant of Divine Timing. When the timing is right, I unify the right people around the right idea and create transformation on the planet. My power is more active when I allow the Universe to set the timing. I wait. I am patient. I trust.

EFT SETUP:

Even though I am afraid to be powerful, I now choose to fully step into my power and allow the Universe to serve me while I serve it, and I deeply and completely love and accept myself.

NOVEMBER 23, 2022 – NEW MOON

 Sagittarius 1 degree, 37 minutes

Gate 34 – The Gate of Power

New Moon energy invites us to explore how we can deepen our alignment with our intentions and asks us to focus on what we want to grow and expand on in our lives.

The definition of true power is changing and healing. Power is not seized, usurped, or forced. True power lies in our ability to respond to the needs of the world. Power is rooted in our ability to gather our resources and to unify towards a common goal.

This New Moon invites us to explore our definition of power and to make sure that we are using power to serve the world from a place of sufficient and trust. We are initiated into a new, healthy definition of power and we are exploring, during this lunar cycle, exactly what we need to do to step into our power.

 CHALLENGE:

To learn to trust in right timing. To not "jump the gun" on an idea, but rather to wait and see what shows up so that your timing is aligned and you're not wasting effort pushing something that is not ready yet.

OPTIMAL EXPRESSION:

The ability to respond to opportunities to unify the right people around a transformative and powerful idea when the timing and circumstances are correct.

UNBALANCED EXPRESSION:

Feeling exhausted, powerless, and frustrated from trying to make your ideas happen when the timing is not right yet. Failing to take stock of your readiness or the readiness of others before launching a new idea or project and feeling perpetually frustrated because it never turns out the way you hoped.

CONTEMPLATIONS:

How are you leveraging your power and energy? Are you doing things that are not bringing you closer to your dreams? What things do you need to stop doing in order to create a space for what you truly want?

What is your definition of power? Do you feel powerful? What can you do to be more powerful in your life?

What do you need to do to deepen your trust in the Universe? Are you showing up and doing your part in your life?

AFFIRMATION:

I trust the Universe to deliver to me the perfect opportunities to fulfill my dreams and intentions. I watch and wait for signs that clearly show me the next step. I know that my true power is in co-creation with the Universe, and I know that Divine Mind has the perfect path for me.

NOVEMBER 28, 2022

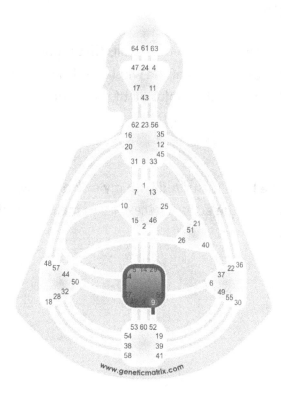

www.geneticmatrix.com

GATE 9: CONVERGENCE

CHALLENGE:

The energy is about learning where to place your focus. When we work with the energy of this Gate, we have to learn to see the trees AND the forest. This Gate can make us seem blind to the big picture and we can lose our focus by getting stuck going down a rabbit hole.

JOURNAL QUESTIONS:

Where am I putting my energy and attention? Is it creating the growth that I am seeking?

What do I need to focus on?

Is my physical environment supporting my staying focused?

Do I have a practice that supports me sustaining my focus? What can I do to increase my focus?

AFFIRMATION:

I place my focus and attention on the details that support my creative manifestation. I am clear. I easily see the parts of the whole, and I know exactly what to focus on to support my evolution and the evolution of the world.

EFT SETUP:

Even though I have been frustrated with my lack of focus, I now choose to be clear, stay focused, and take the actions necessary to create my intentions.

DECEMBER 4, 2022

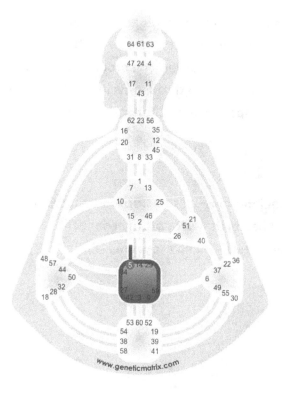

www.geneticmatrix.com

GATE 5: CONSISTENCY

CHALLENGE:

To learn to craft order, habits, and rhythm that support alignment, connection, and the flow of Life Force energy and the fulfillment of purpose. To become skilled at staying in tune with consistent habits and alignment that support your growth and evolution no matter what is going on around you. Aligning with natural order and staying attuned to the unfolding of the flow of the natural world.

JOURNAL QUESTIONS:

What do I need to do to create habits that fuel my energy and keep me vital and feeling connected to myself and Source?

What habits do I have that might not be serving my highest expression? How can I change those habits?

What kind of environment do I need to cultivate to support my rhythmic nature?

AFFIRMATION:

Consistency gives me power. When I am aligned with my own natural rhythm and the rhythm of life around me, I cultivate strength and connection with Source, and I am a beacon of stability and order. The order I hold is the touchstone, the returning point of love, that is sustained through cycles of change. The rhythms I maintain set the standard for compassionate action in the world.

EFT SETUP:

Even though I feel nervous/scared/worried about waiting for Divine Timing, I now choose to create habits that support my connection with Source while I wait, and I deeply and completely love and accept myself.

DECEMBER 8, 2021 – FULL MOON

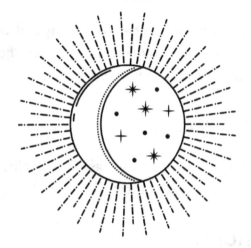

Gemini 16 degrees, 1 minute

Gate 35 – The Gate of Experience

Full moon energy invites us to explore what we need to release and let go of in order to stay in alignment with our intentions.

We are still in a lunar cycle that is inviting us into an exploration of our power. Our power flows, not only from what we have to give and share on the material plane, but also from our experience. This Full Moon is asking us to explore where we may be down-playing the wisdom gleaned from our experiences.

We are releasing anything that causes us to de-value our wisdom and the knowingness that comes from having walked through previous cycles of transformation.

CHALLENGE:

To learn to value your own wisdom and experience. To share the story of your experiences with others. To trust that you know how to know and to use that understanding to face and embrace change and new circumstances with grace.

OPTIMAL EXPRESSION:

The ability to know which experiences are worthy and worthwhile. To partake in the right experience and to share your knowledge from the experience for the sake of changing the story of what is possible in the world.

UNBALANCED EXPRESSION:

To be jaded and unwilling to try new things. To not value your own experience and to fail to share what you know with others.

CONTEMPLATIONS:

What is going on in your life right now that you would like to change?

In your current manifestations, what experiences would you like to avoid duplicating? How can that understanding help you get clear about your creation? What experiences do you need to focus on and align with?

AFFIRMATION:

I choose the kinds of experiences I desire. My feelings about my experiences show me what is correct for me. I am responsible for my own choices and my own happiness, and no one creates experiences for me that I do not choose.

DECEMBER 9, 2022

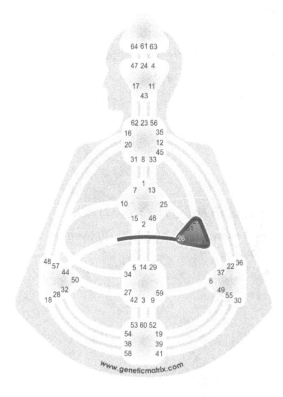

GATE 26: INTEGRITY

CHALLENGE:

To learn to value your right place and your value enough to act as if you are precious. To heal past traumas and elevate your self-worth. To trust in support enough to do the right thing and to nurture yourself so that you have more to give.

JOURNAL QUESTIONS:

Where might I be experiencing a breech in my moral identity, physical, resource, or energy integrity?

What do I need to do to bring myself back into integrity?

When I act without integrity, can it be traumatic?

What trauma do I have that I need to heal?

How can I rewrite that story of my trauma as an initiation back into my true value?

What do I need to do right now to nurture myself and to replenish my value?

AFFIRMATION:

I am a unique, valuable, and irreplaceable part of the Cosmic Plan. I am always supported in fulfilling my right place. I take care of my body, my energy, my values, and my resources so that I have more to share with the world. I claim and defend my value and fully live in the story of who I am with courage.

EFT SETUP:

Even though I am afraid to share my Truth, I now choose to speak my truth clearly and confidently, and I deeply and completely love and accept myself.

DECEMBER 15, 2022

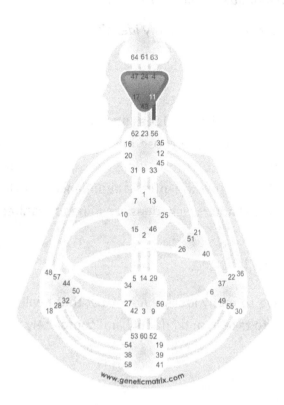

www.geneticmatrix.com

GATE 11: THE CONCEPTUALIST

CHALLENGE:

To sort through and manage all the ideas and inspiration you hold. To trust that the ideas that are yours will show up for you in an actionable way. To value yourself enough to value the ideas you have and to wait for the right people to share those ideas with.

JOURNAL QUESTIONS:

What do I do with inspiration when I receive it?

Do I know how to serve as a steward for my ideas? Or do I feel pressure to try to force them into form?

How much do I value myself? Am I valuing my ideas?

Do I trust the Universe? Do I trust that the ideas that are mine to take action on will manifest in my life according to my Human Design Type and Strategy?

What can I do to manage the pressure I feel to manifest my ideas?

Am I trying to prove my value with my ideas?

AFFIRMATION:

I am a Divine Vessel of inspiration. Ideas flow to me constantly. I protect and nurture these ideas knowing that my purpose in life is to share ideas and inspiration with others. I use the power of these ideas to stimulate my imagination and the imagination of others. I trust the infinite abundance and alignment of the Universe and I wait for signs to know which ideas are mine to manifest.

EFT SETUP:

Even though I have so many ideas, I now trust that I will know exactly what action to take and when to take it, and I deeply and completely love and accept myself.

DECEMBER 20, 2022

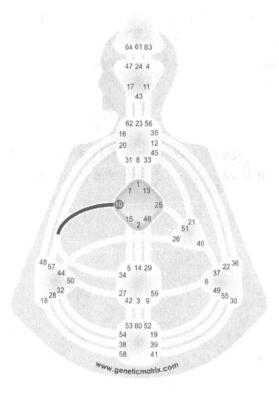

GATE 10: SELF-LOVE

CHALLENGE:

To learn to love yourself. To learn to take responsibility for your own creations.

JOURNAL QUESTIONS:

Do I love myself?

What can I do to deepen my self-love?

Where can I find evidence of my lovability in my life right now?

What do I need to do to take responsibility for situations I hate in my life right now? What needs to change?

Where am I holding blame or victimhood in my life? How could I turn that energy around?

AFFIRMATION:

I am an individuated aspect of the Divine. I am born of Love. My nature is to Love and be Loved. I am in the full flow of giving and receiving Love. I know that the quality of Love that I have for myself, sets the direction for what I attract into my life. I am constantly increasing the quality of love I experience and share with the world.

EFT SETUP:

Even though I struggle with loving myself, I now choose to be open to discovering how to love myself anyway, and I deeply and completely love and accept myself.

DECEMBER 23, 2022 – NEW MOON

 Capricorn 1 degree, 32 minutes
Gate 10 – The Gate of Self-Love

New Moon energy invites us to explore how we can deepen our alignment with our intentions and asks us to focus on what we want to grow and expand on in our lives.

The previous lunar cycle invited us to explore how we can awaken our innate power. We continue this cycle with an exploration of the relationship between our power and our self-love. You cannot be powerful without self-love. Power without self-love leaves us rooted in hidden agendas that strive to prove our love-worthiness. This is the fast track to losing or mis-using our power.

Self-love has nothing to prove. It is inherently self-empowered and allows us to turn our attention to creating waves of self-love and self-empowerment for others.

This lunar cycle invites us to fall madly in love with ourselves and to look at where we may be holding ourselves back or blocking the flow of Love into our lives.

 CHALLENGE:

To learn to love yourself. To learn to take responsibility for your own creations.

OPTIMAL EXPRESSION:

To see your love for yourself as the source of your true creative power. To take all the actions necessary to nurture yourself, set good boundaries, and to embrace an empowered mindset that disallows victim consciousness.

UNBALANCED EXPRESSION:

To question your lovability, struggle to prove your love-worthiness, to give up and settle for less than what you deserve to blame others for your circumstances and situations. Victim consciousness.

CONTEMPLATIONS:

What old energies and "victim stories" do I need to release?

What does being powerful mean to me, and what do I need to do to be more empowered?

Make a list of all the things you love about yourself. Write yourself a beautiful love letter and read it out loud to yourself in the mirror.

What choices and directions could you take that would be in alignment with your self-love?

AFFIRMATION:

I honor the miracle that I am. I am a unique Divine Creation and I know there is no one like me in this world. I make choices and take actions that are honoring of my Divine Magnificence, and I surround myself with people who support me, nurture me, inspire me, and lift me up. I am powerful and in charge of my Life Direction. I make choices that allow me to fulfill my Divine Potential and in being the fullest expression of myself as myself, I create the space for others to do the same.

DECEMBER 26, 2022

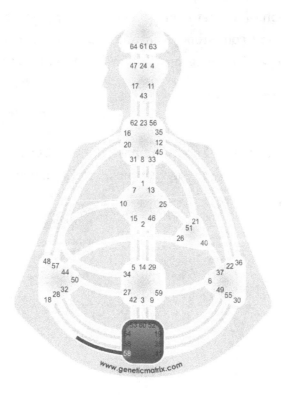

GATE 58: THE GATE OF JOY

CHALLENGE:

To follow the drive to create the fulfillment of your potential. To learn to craft a talent and make it consummate through joyful learning and repetition. To learn to embrace joy as a vital force of creative power without guilt or denial.

JOURNAL QUESTIONS:

What brings me the greatest joy?

How can I deepen my practice of joy?

How can I create more joy in my life?

What keeps me from fulfilling my potential and my talent?

What am I afraid of?

AFFIRMATION:

I am a consummate curator of my own talent. I use my joy to drive me to embody the fun expression of all that I am. I practice as my path to excellency. I know that from repetition and consistency comes a more skillful expression of my talent. I embrace learning and growing, and I commit to the full expression of my joy.

EFT SETUP:

Even though it is hard to let go of the past, I now choose to release it and embrace all the joy that is available to me right now, and I deeply and completely love and accept myself.

DECEMBER 31, 2022

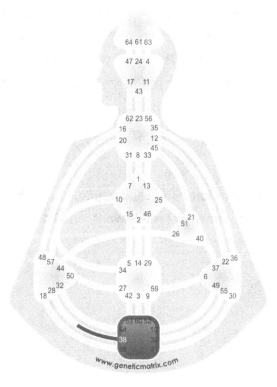

GATE 38: THE VISIONARY

CHALLENGE:

To experience challenge as a way of knowing what is worth fighting for. To turn the story of struggle into a discovery of meaning and to let the power of what you discover serve as a foundation for a strong vision of transformation that brings dreams into manifested form.

JOURNAL QUESTIONS:

Do I know what is worth committing to and fighting for in my life?

Do I have a dream that I am sharing with the world?

Do I know how to use my struggles and challenges as the catalyst for creating deeper meaning in the world? In my life?

AFFIRMATION:

My challenges, struggles, and adventures have taught me about what is truly valuable in life. I use my understandings to hold a vision of what else is possible for the world. I am aligned with the values that reflect the preciousness of life, and I sustain a vision for a world that is aligned with Heart. My steadfast commitment to my vision inspires others to join me in creating a world of equitable, sustainable peace.

EFT SETUP:

Even though things seem hard and challenging, I now choose to use my challenges to help me get clear about what I really want, and I deeply and completely love and accept myself.

JANUARY 6, 2023

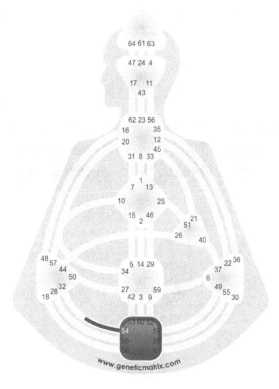

www.geneticmatrix.com

GATE 54: DIVINE INSPIRATION

CHALLENGE:

To learn to be a conduit for Divine Inspiration. To be patient and to wait for alignment and right timing before taking action. To be at peace with stewardship for ideas and to learn to trust the divine trajectory of an inspiration.

JOURNAL QUESTIONS:

What do I do to get inspired?

How do I interface with my creative muse?

Is there anything I need to do or prepare in order to be ready for the next step in the manifestation of my dream or inspiration?

How will I know when I am inspired? Will I feel it in my body?

AFFIRMATION:

I am a Divine Conduit for inspiration. Through me new ideas about creating sustainability and peace on the planet are born. I tend to my inspirations, give them love and energy, and prepare the way for their manifestations in the material world.

EFT SETUP:

Even though I am afraid my dreams will not come true, I now choose to dream wildly and trust that my dreams will come true. All I have to do is focus my mind, trust and know that all will unfold perfectly, and I deeply and completely love and accept myself."

JANUARY 6, 2023 – FULL MOON

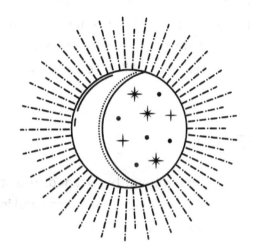

 Cancer 16 degrees, 21 minutes
Gate 53 – The Gate of Starting

Full moon energy invites us to explore what we need to release and let go of in order to stay in alignment with our intentions.

There is a little bit of irony with this Full Moon. Full Moons are all about clearing and releasing and, yet this Full Moon invites us to explore the theme of getting started. We cannot start or begin anything with great momentum if we are not ready or if we are engaging in the relationship with whatever it is we are starting with hidden agendas.

We have to look to the New Moon to explore what we are releasing this lunar cycle. With the New Moon highlighting the Gate 10, the Gate of Self-Love, we see that this Full Moon is lovingly encouraging you to begin anew, to let go of any old narrative or experiences that block you from starting fresh, with a new perspective, a new appreciation for yourself, and with deep reverence and self-love for who you are.

This Full Moon brings us a powerful call to trust that the right things (the things that are ours to initiate) will find us. All we have to do is wait and trust that the things that are ours to "do" will call us out.

CHALLENGE:

To learn which ideas are yours to start and to trust that you will attract the right people and the right parameters to help to finish what you start. To be gentle with yourself if you don't always finish what you start. To give yourself permission to learn from the starting process and to see your ability to begin something as your gift, not your weakness.

OPTIMAL EXPRESSION:

The ability to sit with inspiration and be attuned to what the Inspiration wants and needs. To launch the initiation sequence for an idea and initiate it and then let the idea follow its right course with trust in the flow.

UNBALANCED EXPRESSION:

To feel desperate or frenetic around bringing all of your ideas to fruition. To beat yourself up for not finishing what you start. To push yourself to finish what you started and to feel shame or guilt that you can't follow through.

CONTEMPLATIONS:

What messages did I receive growing up about finishing things? How have those messages shaped my perception of my ability to start things? What needs to be healed, released, aligned, or brought to my awareness for me to embrace my gift of being good at starting things.

AFFIRMATION:

I wait and start things according to my strategy. I allow for the energy of new beginnings and trust that when I live my strategy, all the key pieces to complete my creative process will magically align.

JANUARY 11, 2023

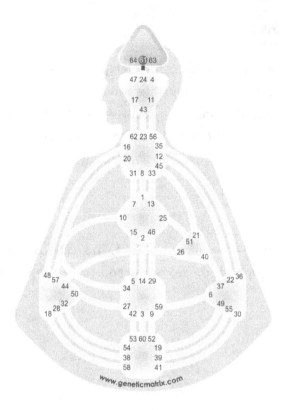

www.geneticmatrix.com

GATE 61: WONDER

CHALLENGE:

To not get lost in trying to answer or figure out why. To maintain a state of wonder. To not let the pressure of trying to know keep you from being present.

JOURNAL QUESTIONS:

What do I do to maintain my sense of wonder?

How can I deepen my awe of the magnificence of the Universe?

What old thoughts, patterns, and beliefs do I need to release in order to align with my knowingness and to trust my "delusional confidence" as a powerful creative state?

What greater perspectives on the events of my life can I see?

What are the greatest lessons I've learned from my pain?

How do I use these lessons to expand my self-expression?

AFFIRMATION:

I have a direct connection to a cosmic perspective that gives me an expanded view of the meaning of the events in my life and the lives of others. I see the wonder and innocence of life and stay present in a constant state of awe. I am innocent and pure in my understanding of the world and my innocence is the source of my creative alignment.

EFT SETUP:

Even though I do not know all the answers, I now choose to surrender and trust that I am being loved, supported, and nurtured by the Infinite Loving Source that is the Universe.

JANUARY 17, 2023

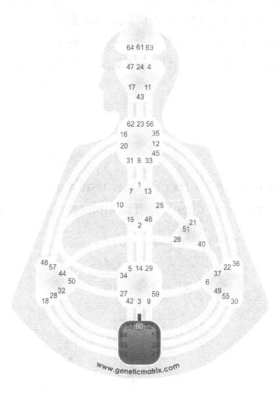

GATE 60: CONSERVATION

CHALLENGE:

To not let the fear of loss overwhelm your resourcefulness. To learn to find what is working and focus on it instead of looking at the loss and disruption.

JOURNAL QUESTIONS:

What change am I resisting?

What am I afraid of?

What are the things in my life that are working that I need to focus on?

Is my fear of loss holding me back?

AFFIRMATION:

I am grateful for all the transformation and change in my life. I know that disruption is the catalyst for my growth. I am able to find the blessings of the past and incorporate them in my innovative vision for the future. I am optimistic about the future, and I transform the world by growing what works.

EFT SETUP:

Even though it is hard to let go of things that did not work, I now release all the clutter from the past, and I deeply and completely love, accept and trust myself.

JANUARY 21, 2022 – NEW MOON

 Aquarius 1 degree, 32 minutes
Gate 60 – The Gate of Conservation

New Moon energy invites us to explore how we can deepen our alignment with our intentions and asks us to focus on what we want to grow and expand on in our lives.

Conservatism isn't necessarily about resisting forward momentum. It is about noting what IS working and building upon it. It is also about gratitude and an honest exploration of the foundation upon which you've built your life.

This New Moon cycle starts with a powerful call to take stock of all that you have and to be grateful. It is also a call to explore what is good and right in your life and to build upon it. Expand and grow what you already know is working.

This isn't resistance or holding back. Innovation is founded on gratitude and deliberate construction rooted in an awareness of what is come before. It is time for us to move forward with great deliberation and bring with us all the blessings and lessons from the past.

 ## CHALLENGE:

To learn to use gratitude as a gateway for innovation. To know that you truly cannot change an experience that you hate. To be highly adaptable by virtue of appreciating what you have. To learn to let go of your old, fixed ideas and embrace the new.

OPTIMAL EXPRESSION:

The ability to find the blessings in transformation. Optimism. To know how to focus on what is working instead of what is not.

UNBALANCED EXPRESSION:

To be ungrateful and bitter. To focus on what you do not have as opposed to what you do have. To hold on to old ideas so tightly that you cannot see innovative options in front of you.

CONTEMPLATIONS:

What things might you need to conserve for the sake of the future? Do you need to change your financial, relationship, health, work, or spiritual habits? If so, how?

Are there any old habits, circumstances, or situations that you need to release to support you in aligning your energy?

Do you need to improve your focus to gain forward momentum? If so, what changes in your daily habits do you need to make to improve your focus?

AFFIRMATION:

I am committed to creating a life that is in alignment with my dreams. I courageously release anything that no longer serves me and I conserve my resources wisely. I know that I am fully supported and that I have been given everything I need to move forward in a powerful way.

SUMMARY

Your Quantum Human Design is your key to understanding your energy, your Life Purpose, your Life Path, and your Soul's Journey in this lifetime. You are a once-in-a-lifetime cosmic event and the fulfillment of your potential and purpose is the greatest gift you can give the world.

I hope this year has been revolutionary for you and that you re-connected with the True story of Who You Are and the power and possibility of your very special life.

If you need additional support and resources to help you on your life path and soul's journey, please visit www.quantumalignmentsystem.com, where you can find Specialists and Practitioners who will help you understand the story of your Human Design chart, coach you, and help you get to the root of any pain, blocks, or limiting beliefs that may be keeping you from enjoying your Life Story. There are all kinds of free goodies, videos, e-books, and resources to help you on your way!

Thank you again for being YOU! We are who we are because you are who you are!

From my Heart to Yours,

Karen

ABOUT THE AUTHOR

Karen Curry Parker is an expert in Quantum Human Design and developed a system to help explore the relationship between Quantum Physics and Human Design. She's the creator of the Quantum Conversations, Amplify!, and Cosmic Revolution podcasts with over 90,000 downloads in less than twelve months and two systems of Human Design: Quantum Human Design™ and the Quantum Alignment System™. Multiple news outlets, radio shows, and tele-summits have featured her work on their programs.

Karen is also the author of numerous bestselling books all designed to help you create the life you were destined to live and find and embrace the purpose of your existence.

Karen is available for private consultations, keynote talks, and to conduct in-house seminars and workshops. You can reach her at Karen@QuantumAlignmentSystem.com.

To run your chart with the new Quantum Human Design language visit:

> www.FreeHumanDesignChart.com

To find out more about Quantum Alignment visit:

> www.QuantumAlignmentSystem.com

For more great books on Human Design, please visit our online store at

books.gracepointpublishing.com

If you enjoyed reading *2022 Quantum Human Design Evolution Guide* and purchased it through an online retailer, please return to the site and write a review to help others find this book.

CPSIA information can be obtained
at www.ICGtesting.com
Printed in the USA
LVHW021237190122
708794LV00008B/233

9 781955 272070